Step Up & Into

Windows PowerShell 4.0

Smart Brain Training Solutions

PUBLISHED BY

Smart Brain Training Solutions
PO Box 362
East Olympia, WA 98540-0362

Cover Design: Creative Designs Ltd.
Editorial Development: Andover Publishing Solutions
Technical Review: L & L Technical Content Services

You can provide feedback related to this book by emailing the author at williamstanek@aol.com. Please use the name of the book as the subject line.

Table of Contents

Introduction

Step Up & Into Windows PowerShell 4.0 is written for anyone who is already familiar with Windows PowerShell and wants to learn the new and changed features of Windows PowerShell 3.0 and Windows PowerShell 4.0. Not only does this book zero in on what's new and changed, it provides the necessary context for you to understand how the new features and changes affect the way you use Windows PowerShell.

I don't recommend buying this book if you've already bought or are planning to buy *Windows PowerShell: The Personal Trainer for Windows PowerShell 3.0 and Windows PowerShell 4.0*. The reason for this is that the books cover essentially the same material. *Windows PowerShell: The Personal Trainer* provides an in-depth, authoritative look at Windows PowerShell, including what's new and the important changes for Windows PowerShell 3.0 and Windows PowerShell 4.0. *Step Up & Into Windows PowerShell 4.0* focuses on what's new and changed but also gives you the necessary background to work successfully with these new and changed features.

What Conventions Are Used in This Book?

In this book, I've used a variety of elements to help keep the text clear and easy to follow. You'll find code terms and listings in `monospace` type, except when I tell you to actually enter a command. In that case, the command appears in **bold** type. When I introduce and define a new term, I put it in *italics*.

This book also has notes, tips and other sidebar elements that provide additional details on points that need emphasis.

Other Resources

Although some books are offered as all-in-one guides, there's simply no way one book can do it all. This book is intended to be used as a concise and easy-to-use resource. It covers everything you need to perform core tasks with Windows PowerShell, but it is by no means exhaustive.

As you encounter new topics, take the time to practice what you've learned and read about. Seek additional information as necessary to get the practical experience and knowledge that you need.

I truly hope you find that *Step Up & Into Windows PowerShell 4.0* helps you use Windows PowerShell successfully and effectively.

Thank you,

William R. Stanek

(williamstanek@aol.com)

Chapter 1. Getting Started

Windows PowerShell 3.0 and Windows PowerShell 4.0 are enhanced and extended editions of the original implementations of PowerShell. The changes are dramatic, and they improve both the performance capabilities of PowerShell and its versatility. You can do things with PowerShell 3.0 and PowerShell 4.0 that you simply could not do with earlier versions, and you can perform standard tasks in much more efficient ways than before. The discussion that follows explores PowerShell options and configurations and also provides tips for using the command history.

Windows and Windows Server operating systems are released with a specific version of Windows PowerShell:

- Windows PowerShell 4.0 is built into Windows 8.1 and Windows Server 2012 Release 2 (R2). Also, you can install PowerShell 4.0 on computers running Windows 7 with Service Pack 1 or later, and Windows Server 2008 R2 with Service Pack 1 or later by installing Windows Management Framework 4.0.
- Windows PowerShell 3.0 is built into Windows 8 and Windows Server 2012. Also, you can install PowerShell 3.0 on computers running Windows 7 with Service Pack 1 or later, Windows Server 2008 R2 with Service Pack 1 or later, and Windows Server 2008 with Service Pack 2 or later by installing Windows Management Framework 3.0.

The prerequisites for using Windows PowerShell depend on the version you are working with:

- Windows PowerShell 4.0 requires a full installation of .NET Framework 4.5. Windows 8.1 and Windows Server 2012 R2 include Microsoft .NET Framework 4.5 by default.

- Windows PowerShell 3.0 requires a full installation of .NET Framework 4. Windows 8 and Windows Server 2012 include Microsoft .NET Framework 4.5 by default, which includes the .NET Framework 4 components.

Also, Windows PowerShell 3.0 and Windows PowerShell 4.0 require:

- WS-Management 3.0, which supports the Windows Remote Management (WinRM) service and the WS-Management (WSMan) protocol.
- Windows Management Instrumentation 3.0 (WMI), which supports PowerShell features that access managed resources through WMI.

REAL WORLD   The Distributed Management Task Force (DMTF) created the Common Information Model (CIM) standard to describe the structure and behavior of managed resources. Windows Management Instrumentation (WMI) is a CIM server service that implements the CIM standard on Windows.

WS-Management (WS-Man) is a protocol for managing communications between a CIM client and a CIM server. WS-Man is based on Simple Object Access Protocol (SOAP), which is implemented using the eXtensible Markup Language (XML).

Windows Remote Management (WinRM) is the Microsoft implementation of the WS-Man protocol on Windows.

These components are included in Windows 8, Windows 8.1, Windows Server 2012, and Windows Server 2012 R2. For other supported operating systems, these components are installed when you install Windows Management Framework 3.0 or Windows Management Framework 4.0 as required. Different builds are available for each version of Windows, in 32-bit and 64-bit editions. See Microsoft TechNet Library Article HH847769 for complete details and links to the required components (http://technet.microsoft.com/en-us/library/hh847769.aspx).

Windows PowerShell has both a command-line environment and a graphical environment for running commands and scripts. The PowerShell console (powershell.exe) is a 32-bit or 64-bit environment for working with PowerShell at the command line. On 32-bit versions of Windows, you'll find the 32-bit executable in the %SystemRoot%\System32\WindowsPowerShell\v1.0 directory. On 64-bit versions of Windows, you'll find the 32-bit executable in the %SystemRoot%\SysWow64\WindowsPowerShell\v1.0 directory and the 64-bit executable in the %SystemRoot%\System32\WindowsPowerShell\v1.0 directory.

> **NOTE** %SystemRoot% refers to the SystemRoot environment variable. The Windows operating system has many environment variables, which are used to refer to user-specific and system-specific values. I'll often refer to environment variables using the standard Windows syntax %VariableName%. In Windows PowerShell, you access and work with environment variables using the Env provider. Providers are discussed in Chapter 4, "Using Providers."

Chapter 2. Working with the Help Documentation

With Windows PowerShell 3.0 and later, help files aren't included with the standard installation and Windows PowerShell displays automatically generated help information by default. If you want to work with the full help documentation, you must either access the help files online or download updated help files to your computer.

Accessing Help Files

When working locally and not in a remote session, you can view help files for cmdlets online in the TechNet Library by adding the –Online parameter whenever you use Get-Help, such as:

```
get-help new-variable -online
```

If a computer doesn't have an Internet connection or you are working in a remote session, you won't be able to get online help and instead will need to rely on the default help files or help files that have been downloaded and installed on the computer. To download and install the current version of help files, enter the following command at an elevated, administrator PowerShell prompt:

```
update-help
```

When you run Update-Help without specifying additional parameters, Windows PowerShell attempts to connect to the Internet and download the help files from Microsoft's website. These actions will only be successful when the computer has a connection to the Internet and the connection isn't blocked by firewall rules or Internet privacy settings.

> **REAL WORLD**   Running Update-Help from an administrator prompt is recommended as a best practice, but it is not required. By default, Update-Help downloads and installs the newest help file for modules available on a computer as well as modules in a remote session. If help files were previously installed, Update-Help only updates the help files that have been modified since they were installed. However, if you run Update-Help with standard permissions, Update-Help will not download or install help files for modules in the PowerShell installation directory, including the Windows PowerShell Core modules. Thus, to ensure help files for all available modules are installed and updated, you must run Windows PowerShell with the Run As Administrator option.

Creating a Central Help Folder

Rather than downloading and installing help files on multiple computers or when computers don't have connections to the Internet, you may want to specify a central help location for your organization and then install help files from this location as required. Installing and using help files from a central location is a two-step process:

1. You use Save-Help to download help files and save them to a specified folder or network share.
2. You use Update-Help to install help files from the central location.

With you are working with Save-Help, you specify the destination path using the –DestinationPath parameter, such as:

```
Save-Help -DestinationPath C:\HelpFiles
```

Or

```
Save-Help -DestinationPath \\Server54\PS_Help
```

As long as the destination paths exist and you have permission to write to the location, you'll be able to save the help files. In these instances, here's how Save-Help works with PowerShell 4.0 and later:

1. The PowerShell modules on the computer to which you are currently logged on as well as the modules in the current remote session determine which help files are used. When you run Save-Help, Save-Help identifies all the PowerShell modules installed on the current computer and in the current session.

2. Next, if the destination folder was previously used to save help files, Save-Help checks the version of the help files in the destination folder. If newer help files are available for the applicable PowerShell modules, Save-Help downloads the new help files and saves them in the destination folder.

> **REAL WORLD**   When you are working in a remote session, there's an important difference between the way Save-Help works with PowerShell 3.0 and PowerShell 4.0. With PowerShell 3.0, the HelpInfoUri property, which identifies the location of help files online by their URL, is not preserved when remoting. Thus, Save-Help works only for modules installed on the local computer and does not apply to modules in the remote session. On the other hand, with PowerShell 4.0, the HelpInfoUri property is preserved when remoting. Thus, Save-Help is able to pass back the location of help files for modules that are installed on the remote computer, which in turn allows you to save help files for the modules installed on the remote computer.

Often, you'll need to pass in credentials to update help files. Use the –Credential parameter to do this. In the following example, you specify that the WilliamS account in the ImaginedL domain should be used to perform the update task:

```
Save-Help -DestinationPath \\Server54\PS_Help
-Credential ImaginedL\Williams
```

When you run the command, you are prompted for the password for the WilliamS account. The account's credentials are then used to write to the destination path.

Once you save help files to a central location, you can write the help files to any computer in your organization and in this way make the help files available locally. To do this, run Update-Help and use the –SourcePath parameter to specify the source location for the help files, such as:

```
Update-Help -SourcePath \\Server54\PS_Help
-Credential ImaginedL\Williams
```

Help files are language specific. Update-Help and Save-Help create language-specific files for all languages and locales configured on your management computer. Thus, if the Region And Language settings for your management computer specify the current locale as US English, the help commands create and work with the US English help files by default.

When you are working in an enterprise where computers are deployed using different languages, locales or both, it is important to note that a problem can occur when help files are saved with language or culture settings that are different from the language and culture settings of your management computer. For example, if help files were saved with the current locale set as US English but you are working with a computer with the current locale set as UK English, you won't be able to retrieve the help files for that locale from the source location. An easy work around is to save help files to the central share using computers that have the appropriate languages and cultures configured.

Chapter 3. Using Snap-ins

Windows PowerShell snap-ins are .NET programs that are compiled into DLL files. Snap-ins can include providers and cmdlets. PowerShell providers are .NET programs that provide access to specialized data stores so that you can access the data stores from the command line. Before using a provider, you must install the related snap-in and add it to your Windows PowerShell session.

Snap-in Essentials

When you add a snap-in, the providers and cmdlets that it contains are immediately available for use in the current session. To ensure that a snap-in is available in all future sessions, add the snap-in via your profile. You can also use the Export-Console cmdlet to save the names of snap-ins to a console file. If you start a console by using the console file, the named snap-ins are available.

To save the snap-ins from a session in a console file (.psc1), use the Export-Console cmdlet. For example, to save the snap-ins in the current session configuration to the MyConsole.psc1 file in the current directory, enter the following command:

```
export-console MyConsole
```

The following command starts PowerShell with the MyConsole.psc1 console file:

```
powershell.exe -psconsolefile MyConsole.psc1
```

You can list the available snap-ins by entering **get-pssnapin**. To find the snap-in for each Windows PowerShell provider, enter the following command:

```
get-psprovider | format-list name, pssnapin
```

To list the cmdlets in a snap-in, enter

```
get-command -module SnapinName
```

where SnapinName is the name of the snap-in you want to examine.

PowerShell Core Commands

Beginning with PowerShell 3.0, the core commands are packaged in modules rather than snap-ins. The only exception is Microsoft.PowerShell.Core, a snap-in that contains providers and cmdlets used to manage the basic features of Windows PowerShell. Microsoft.PowerShell.Core includes the Alias, Environment, FileSystem, Function, Registry, and Variable providers and basic cmdlets like Add-History, Add-PSSnapin, Get-Command, Get-Help and New-Module.

> **NOTE** A key difference between modules and snap-ins is that while modules can add all types of commands to the working environment, including cmdlets, functions, providers, variables, aliases, and PowerShell drives, snap-ins can only add cmdlets and providers.

Microsoft.PowerShell.Core is registered in the operating system and added to the default session whenever you start Windows PowerShell. To use snap-ins that you create or obtain from other sources, you must register them and add them to your console session. To find registered snap-ins (other than the built-in snap-ins) on your system or to verify that an additional snap-in is registered, enter the following command:

```
get-pssnapin -registered
```

Adding and Removing Snap-ins

You can add a registered snap-in to the current session by using Add-PSSnapin. The basic syntax is to follow Add-PSSnapin with the name of the snap-in to add. For example, if you want to add the ADRMS.PS.Admin snap-in, you would enter **add-pssnapin adrms.ps.admin**.

Once you add the snap-in, its providers and cmdlets are available in the console session. If you add the necessary Add-PSSnapin commands to a relevant profile, you can be sure that modules you want to use are always loaded.

To remove a Windows PowerShell snap-in from the current session, use Remove-PSSnapin to remove the snap-in from the session. The basic syntax is to follow Remove-PSSnapin with the name of the snap-in to remove, such as Remove-PSSnapin ADRMS.PS.ADMIN. Although the removed snap-in is still loaded, the providers and cmdlets that it supports are no longer available.

Checking for Snap-in Availability

When you are performing administrative tasks or creating scripts for later use, you'll may want to ensure that a particular PowerShell snap-in is available before you try to use its features. The easiest way to do this is to attempt to perform the action or run a script only if the snap-in is available. Consider the following example:

```
if (get-pssnapin -name ADRMS.PS.Admin -erroraction
silentlycontinue)
  {

  Code to execute if the snap-in is available.

} else {

  Code to execute if the snap-in is not available.

}
```

Here, when the ADRMS.PS.Admin snap-in is available, the statement in parentheses evaluates to True, and any code in the related script block is executed. When the ADRMS.PS.Admin snap-in is not available, the statement in parentheses evaluates to False, and any code in the Else statement is executed. Note also that I set the –ErrorAction parameter to SilentlyContinue so that error messages aren't written to the output if the snap-in is not found.

> **TIP** The same technique can be used with providers and modules.

Chapter 4. Using Providers

The data that a provider exposes appears in a drive that you can browse much like you browse a hard drive, allowing you to view, search though, and manage related data. To list all providers that are available, type **Get-PSProvider**. Table 4-1 lists the built-in providers. Note the drives associated with each provider.

TABLE 4-1 Built-In PowerShell Providers

PROVIDER	DATA ACCESSED & DRIVE
Alias	Windows PowerShell aliases {Alias}
Certificate	X509 certificates for digital signatures {Cert}
Environment	Windows environment variables {Env}
FileSystem	File system drives, directories, and files {C, D, E, …}
Function	Windows PowerShell functions {Function}
Registry	Windows registry

	{HKLM, HKCU}
Variable	Windows PowerShell variables {Variable}
WSMan	WS-Management {WSMan}

PowerShell includes a set of cmdlets that are specifically designed to manage the items in the data stores that are exposed by providers. You use these cmdlets in the same ways to manage all the different types of data that the providers make available to you. Table 4-2 provides an overview of these cmdlets.

TABLE 4-2 Cmdlets for Working with Data Stores

CMDLET	DESCRIPTION
Get-PSDrive	Gets all or specified PowerShell drives in the current console. This includes logical drives on the computer, drives mapped to network shares, and drives exposed by Windows PowerShell providers. Get-PSDrive does not get Windows mapped drives that are added or created after you open PowerShell. However, you can map drives using New-PSDrive, and those drives will be available. Get-PSDrive [[-Name] *Strings*] [-PSProvider *Strings*] [-Scope *String*] [-UseTransaction] Get-PSDrive [[-LiteralName] *Strings*] [-PSProvider *Strings*] [-Scope *String*] [-UseTransaction]

CMDLET	DESCRIPTION
New-PSDrive	Creates a PowerShell drive that is mapped to a location in a data store, which can include a shared network folder, a local directory, or a registry key. The drive is available only in the current PowerShell console. New-PSDrive [-Name] *String* [-PSProvider] *String* [-Root] *String* [-Credential *Credential*] [-Description *String*] [-Scope *String*] [-UseTransaction]
Remove-PSDrive	Removes a PowerShell drive that you added to the current console session. You cannot delete Windows drives or mapped network drives created by using other methods. Remove-PSDrive [[-Name] *Strings* [-Force] [-PSProvider *Strings*] [-Scope *String*] [-UseTransaction] Remove-PSDrive [[-LiteralName] *Strings* [-Force] [-PSProvider *Strings*] [-Scope *String*] [-UseTransaction]
Get-ChildItem	Gets the items and child items in one or more specified locations. Get-ChildItem [[-Path] *Strings*] [[-Filter] *String*] [AddtlParams] Get-ChildItem [[-Filter] *String*] [-LiteralPath] *Strings* [AddtlParams] Get-ChildItem [-Attributes *FileAttribs*] [-Directory] [-File] [-Force] [-Hidden] [-ReadOnly] [-System] [-UseTransaction] AddtlParams= [-Exclude *Strings*] [-Force] [-Include *Strings*] [-Name] [-Recurse] [-UseTransaction]
Get-Item	Gets the item at the specified location. Get-Item [[-LiteralPath] | [-Path]] *Strings* [AddtlParams] AddtlParams= [-Credential *Credential*] [-Exclude *Strings*] [-Filter *String*] [-Force]

CMDLET	DESCRIPTION
	[-Include *Strings*] [-UseTransaction]
New-Item	Creates a new item. New-Item [-Path] *Strings* [AddtlParams] New-Item -Name *String* [AddtlParams] AddtlParams= [-Credential *Credential*] [-Force] [-ItemType *String*] [-Value *Object*] [-UseTransaction]
Set-Item	Changes the value of an item to the value specified in the command. Set-Item [-Path] *Strings* [[-Value] *Object*] [AddtlParams] Set-Item [[-Value] *Object*] –LiteralPath *Strings* [AddtlParams] AddtlParams= [-Credential *Credential*] [-Exclude *Strings*] [-Filter *String*] [-Force] [-Include *Strings*] [-PassThru] [-UseTransaction]
Remove-Item	Deletes the specified item. Remove-Item [-Path] *Strings* [AddtlParams] Remove-Item –LiteralPath *Strings* [AddtlParams] AddtlParams= [-Credential *Credential*] [-Exclude *Strings*] [-Filter *String*] [-Force] [-Include *Strings*] [-Recurse] [-UseTransaction]
Move-Item	Moves an item from one location to another. Move-Item [-Path] *Strings* [[-Destination] *String*] [AddtlParams] Move-Item [[-Destination] *String*] –LiteralPath *Strings* [AddtlParams] AddtlParams= [-Credential *Credential*] [-Exclude *Strings*] [-Filter *String*] [-Force]

CMDLET	DESCRIPTION
	[-Include *Strings*] [-PassThru] [-UseTransaction]
Rename-Item	Renames an item in a Windows PowerShell provider namespace. Rename-Item [-Path] *String* [-NewName] *String* [AddtlParams] Rename-Item [-NewName] *String* -LiteralPath *String* [AddtlParams] AddtlParams= [-Credential *Credential*] [-Force] [-PassThru] [-UseTransaction]
Copy-Item	Copies an item from one location to another within a namespace. Copy-Item [-Path] *Strings* [[-Destination] *String*] [AddtlParams] Copy-Item [[-Destination] *String*] –LiteralPath *Strings* [AddtlParams] AddtlParams= [-Container] [-Credential *Credential*] [-Exclude *Strings*] [-Filter *String*] [-Force] [-Include *Strings*] [-PassThru] [-Recurse] [-UseTransaction]
Clear-Item	Deletes the contents of an item but does not delete the item. Clear-Item [-Path] *Strings* [AddtlParams] Clear-Item –LiteralPath *Strings* [AddtlParams] AddtlParams= [-Credential *Credential*] [-Exclude *Strings*] [-Filter *String*] [-Force] [-Include *Strings*] [-UseTransaction]
Invoke-Item	Performs the default action on the specified item. Invoke-Item [-Path] *Strings* [AddtlParams] Invoke-Item –LiteralPath *Strings* [AddtlParams] AddtlParams= [-Credential *Credential*] [-Exclude *Strings*] [-Filter *String*] [-Include *Strings*] [-UseTransaction]

CMDLET	DESCRIPTION
Clear-ItemProperty	Deletes the value of a property but does not delete the property. Clear-ItemProperty [-Path] *Strings* [-Name] *String* [AddtlParams] Clear-ItemProperty [-Name] *String* –LiteralPath *Strings* [AddtlParams] AddtlParams= [-Credential *Credential*] [-Exclude *Strings*] [-Filter *String*] [-Force] [-Include *Strings*] [-PassThru] [-UseTransaction]
Copy-ItemProperty	Copies a property and value from a specified location to another location. Copy-ItemProperty [-Path] *Strings* [-Destination] *String* [-Name] *String* [AddtlParams] Copy-ItemProperty [-Destination] *String* [-Name] *String* –LiteralPath *Strings* [AddtlParams] AddtlParams= [-Credential *Credential*] [-Exclude *Strings*] [-Filter *String*] [-Force] [-Include *Strings*] [-PassThru] [-UseTransaction]
Get-ItemProperty	Gets the properties of a specified item. Get-ItemProperty [-Path] *Strings* [[-Name] *Strings*] [AddtlParams] Get-ItemProperty [[-Name] *String*] –LiteralPath *Strings* [AddtlParams] AddtlParams= [-Credential *Credential*] [-Exclude *Strings*] [-Filter *String*] [-Include *Strings*] [-UseTransaction]
Move-ItemProperty	Moves a property from one location to another. Move-ItemProperty [-Path] *Strings* [-Destination] *String* [-Name] *Strings* [AddtlParams]

CMDLET	DESCRIPTION
	Move-ItemProperty [-Destination] *String* [-Name] *Strings* –LiteralPath *Strings* [AddtlParams] AddtlParams= [-Credential *Credential*] [-Exclude *Strings*] [-Filter *String*] [-Force] [-Include *Strings*] [-PassThru] [-UseTransaction]
New-ItemProperty	Creates a property for an item and sets its value. New-ItemProperty [-Path] *Strings* [-Name] *String* [AddtlParams] New-ItemProperty [-Name] *String* –LiteralPath *Strings* [AddtlParams] AddtlParams= [-Credential *Credential*] [-Exclude *Strings*] [-Filter *String*] [-Force] [-Include *Strings*] [-Value *Object*] [-UseTransaction]
Remove-ItemProperty	Deletes the specified property and its value from an item. Remove-ItemProperty [-Path] *Strings* [-Name] *Strings* [AddtlParams] Remove-ItemProperty [-Name] *Strings* –LiteralPath *Strings* [AddtlParams] AddtlParams= [-Credential *Credential*] [-Exclude *Strings*] [-Filter *String*] [-Force] [-Include *Strings*] [-UseTransaction]
Rename-ItemProperty	Renames the specified property of an item. Rename-ItemProperty [-Path] *String* [-Name] *String* [-NewName] *String* [AddtlParams] Rename -ItemProperty [-Name] *String* [-NewName] *String* –LiteralPath *String* [AddtlParams] AddtlParams= [-Credential *Credential*] [-Exclude *Strings*] [-Filter *String*] [-Force]

CMDLET	DESCRIPTION
	[-Include *Strings*] [-PassThru] [-UseTransaction]
Set-ItemProperty	Creates or changes the value of the specified property of an item.
	Set-ItemProperty [-Path] *Strings* [-Name] *String* [-Value] *Object* [AddtlParams]
	Set-ItemProperty [-Path] *Strings* -InputObject *Object* [AddtlParams]
	Set-ItemProperty -InputObject *Object* -LiteralPath *Strings* [AddtlParams]
	Set-ItemProperty [-Name] *String* [-Value] *Object* -LiteralPath *Strings* [AddtlParams]
	AddtlParams= [-Credential *Credential*] [-Exclude *Strings*] [-Filter *String*] [-Force] [-Include *Strings*] [-PassThru] [-UseTransaction]

Navigating Provider Drives

Providers deliver consistent access to data. In addition to the built-in cmdlets, providers can:

- Have custom cmdlets that are designed especially for related data.
- Add "dynamic parameters" to the built-in cmdlets that are available only when using the cmdlet with the provider data.

The drive associated with each provider is listed in the default display of Get-PSProvider, but you can get more information about a provider drive by using the Get-PSDrive cmdlet. For example, the Registry provider makes the HKEY_LOCAL_MACHINE root key available as the HKLM drive. To find all the properties of the HKLM drive, enter the following command:

```
get-psdrive hklm | format-list *
```

You can view and navigate through the data in a provider drive just as you would data in a file system drive. To view the contents of a provider drive, use the Get-Item or Get-ChildItem cmdlet. Type the drive name followed by a colon (:). For example, to view the contents of the Function drive, type:

```
get-childitem function:
```

You can view and manage the data in any drive from another drive by including the drive name in the path. For example, to view the HKLM\Software registry key in the HKLM drive from another drive, type:

```
get-childitem hklm:\software
```

To get into the drive, use the Set-Location cmdlet. Remember the colon when specifying the drive path. For example, to change your location to the root of the Function drive, type **set-location function:**. Then, to view the contents of the Function drive, type **get-childitem**.

You can navigate through a provider drive just as you would a hard drive. If the data is arranged in a hierarchy of items within items, use a backslash (\) to indicate a child item. The basic syntax is:

```
Set-location drive:\location\child-location\...
```

For example, to change your location to the HKLM\Software registry key, use a Set-Location command, such as:

```
set-location hklm:\software
```

You can also use relative references to locations. A dot (.) represents the current location. For example, if you are in the C:\Windows\System32 directory and you want to list its files and folders, you can use the following command:

```
get-childitem .\
```

Managing Providers

PowerShell providers are packaged as snap-ins. When PowerShell loads providers, the providers can add dynamic parameters that are available only when the cmdlet is used with that provider. For example, the Certificate drive adds the –CodeSigningCert parameter to the Get-Item and Get-ChildItem cmdlets. You can use this parameter only when you use Get-Item or Get-ChildItem in the Cert drive.

Although you cannot uninstall a provider, you can remove the Windows PowerShell snap-in for the provider from the current session. To remove a provider, use the Remove-PSSnapin cmdlet. This cmdlet does not unload or uninstall providers. It removes all the contents of the snap-in, including providers and cmdlets. This makes the related providers and cmdlets unavailable in the current session.

Another way to remove features made available based on snap-ins is to use the Remove-PSDrive cmdlet to remove a particular drive from the current session. When you remove a drive, the data on the drive is not affected, but the drive is no longer available in the current session.

Often, you'll want to ensure that a particular PowerShell provider or PSDrive is available before you try to work with its features. The easiest way to do this is to attempt to perform the action or run a script only if the provider or PSDrive is available. Consider the following example:

```
If (get-psprovider -psprovider wsman -erroraction
silentlycontinue)
  {

  Code to execute if the provider is available.

} else {

  Code to execute if the provider is not available.

}
```

Here, when the WSMan provider is available, the statement in parentheses evaluates to True, and any code in the related script block is executed. When the WSMan provider is not available, the statement in parentheses evaluates to False, and any code in the Else statement is executed. Note also that I set the –ErrorAction parameter to SilentlyContinue so that error messages aren't written to the output if the provider is not found.

Working with Provider Drives

When you are using provider drives, you might also want to manage content, configure locations, and work with paths. Table 4-3 provides an overview of cmdlets that you can use to perform related tasks.

TABLE 4-3 Cmdlets for Working with Provider Drives

CMDLET	DESCRIPTION
Add-Content	Adds content to the specified item, such as adding words to a file. Add-Content [-Path] *Strings* [-Value] *Objects* [AddtlParams] Add-Content [-Value] *Objects* -LiteralPath *Strings* [AddtlParams] Add-Content [-Encoding {Unknown | String | Unicode | Byte | BigEndianUnicode | UTF8 | UTF7 | UTF32 | Ascii | Default | Oem}] [-Force] [-Stream *String*] [-UseTransaction] AddtlParams= [-Credential *Credential*] [-Exclude *Strings*] [-Filter *String*] [-Force] [-Include *Strings*] [-PassThru] [-UseTransaction]
Clear-Content	Deletes the contents of an item, such as deleting the text from a file, but does not delete the item. Clear-Content [-Path] *Strings* [AddtlParams] Clear-Content -LiteralPath *Strings* [AddtlParams] AddtlParams= [-Credential *Credential*] [-Exclude *Strings*] [-Filter *String*] [-Force] [-Include *Strings*] [-UseTransaction]
Get-Content	Gets the content of the item at the specified location. Get-Content [-Path] *Strings* [AddtlParams] Get-Content -LiteralPath *Strings* [AddtlParams] Get-Content [-Delimiter *String*] [-Encoding {Unknown | String | Unicode | Byte | BigEndianUnicode | UTF8 | UTF7 | UTF32 | Ascii | Default | Oem}] [-Force] [-Raw] [-Stream *String*] [-Wait] [-UseTransaction] AddtlParams= [-Credential *Credential*] [-Exclude *Strings*] [-Filter *String*] [-Force] [-Include *Strings*] [-ReadCount *Count*] [-TotalCount *Count*] [-UseTransaction]

CMDLET	DESCRIPTION
Set-Content	Writes content to an item or replaces the content in an item with new content. Set-Content [-Path] *Strings* [-Value] *Objects* [AddtlParams] Set-Content [-Value] *Objects* -LiteralPath *Strings* [AddtlParams] Set-Content [-Encoding {Unknown | String | Unicode | Byte | BigEndianUnicode | UTF8 | UTF7 | UTF32 | Ascii | Default | Oem}] [-Force] [-Raw] [-Stream *String*] [-Wait] [-UseTransaction] AddtlParams= [-Credential *Credential*] [-Exclude *Strings*] [-Filter *String*] [-Force] [-Include *Strings*] [-PassThru] [-UseTransaction]
Get-Location	Gets information about the current working location. Get-Location [-PSDrive *Strings*] [-PSProvider *Strings*] [-UseTransaction] Get-Location [-Stack] [-StackName *Strings*] [-UseTransaction]
Set-Location	Sets the current working location to a specified location. Set-Location [[-Path] *String*] [-PassThru] [-UseTransaction] Set-Location [-PassThru] -LiteralPath *String* [-UseTransaction] Set-Location [-PassThru] [-StackName *String*] [-UseTransaction]
Push-Location	Adds the current location to the top of a list of locations. ("stack"). Push-Location [[-Path] *String*] [-PassThru] [-StackName *String*] [-UseTransaction] Push-Location [-LiteralPath] *String* [-PassThru] [-StackName *String*] [-UseTransaction]
Pop-Location	Changes the current location to the location most recently pushed onto the stack.

CMDLET	DESCRIPTION
	Pop-Location [-PassThru] [-StackName *String*] [-UseTransaction]
Join-Path	Combines a path and a child-path into a single path. The provider supplies the path delimiters. Join-Path [-Path] *Strings* [-ChildPath] *String* [-Credential *Credential*] [-Resolve] [-UseTransaction]
Convert-Path	Converts a path from a Windows PowerShell path to a Windows PowerShell provider path. Convert-Path [-Path] *Strings* [-UseTransaction] Convert-Path -LiteralPath *Strings* [-UseTransaction]
Split-Path	Returns the specified part of a path. Split-Path -LiteralPath *Strings* [-Credential *Credential*] [-Resolve] [-UseTransaction] Split-Path [-Path] *Strings* [AddtlParams] AddtlParams= [-Credential *Credential*] [-IsAbsolute | -Leaf | -Parent | -NoQualifier | -Qualifier] [-Resolve] [-UseTransaction]
Test-Path	Determines whether all elements of a path exist. Test-Path [-Path] *Strings* [AddtlParams] Test-Path –LiteralPath *Strings* [AddtlParams] Test-Path [-NewerThan *DateTime*] [-OlderThan *DateTime*] AddtlParams= [-Credential *Credential*] [-Exclude *Strings*] [-Filter *String*] [-Include *Strings*] [-IsValid] [-PathType {<Any> | <Container> | <Leaf>}] [-UseTransaction]

CMDLET	DESCRIPTION
Resolve-Path	Resolves the wildcard characters in a path and displays the path's contents. Resolve-Path [-Path] *Strings* [-Credential *Credential*] [AddtlParams] Resolve-Path –LiteralPath *Strings* [AddtlParams] AddtlParams= [-Credential *Credential*] [-Relative] [-UseTransaction]

Setting the Working Location

The currently selected provider drive determines what data store you are working with. The default data store is the file system, and the default path within the file system is the profile directory for the currently logged-on user (in most cases).

The current working location is the location that Windows PowerShell uses if you do not supply an explicit path to the item or location that is affected by the command. Typically, this is a directory on a hard drive accessed through the FileSystem provider. All commands are processed from this working location unless another path is explicitly provided.

PowerShell keeps track of the current working location for each drive even when the drive is not the current drive. This allows you to access items from the current working location by referring only to the drive of another location. For example, suppose that your current working location is C:\Scripts\PowerShell. Then you use the following command to change your current working location to the HKLM drive:

```
Set-Location HKLM:
```

Although your current location is now the HKLM drive, you can still access items in the C:\Scripts\PowerShell directory by using the C drive, as shown in the following example:

```
Get-ChildItem C:
```

PowerShell retains the information that your current working location for the C drive is the C:\Scripts\PowerShell directory, so it retrieves items from that directory. The results would be the same if you ran the following command:

```
Get-ChildItem C:\Scripts\PowerShell
```

You can use the Get-Location command to determine the current working location, and you can use the Set-Location command to set the current working location. For example, the following command sets the current working location to the Scripts directory of the C drive:

```
Set-Location c:\scripts
```

After you set the current working location, you can still access items from other drives simply by including the drive name (followed by a colon) in the command, as shown in the following example:

```
Get-ChildItem HKLM:\software
```

This example retrieves a list of items in the Software container of the HKEY Local Machine hive in the registry.

You use special characters to represent the current working location and its parent location. To represent the current working location, you use a single period. To represent the parent of the current working location, you use two periods. For example, the following command specifies the PowerShell subdirectory in the current working location:

```
Get-ChildItem .\PowerShell
```

If the current working location is C:\Scripts, this command returns a list of all the items in C:\Scripts\PowerShell. However, if you use two periods, the parent directory of the current working location is used, as shown in the following example:

```
Get-ChildItem ..\Data
```

In this case, PowerShell treats the two periods as the C drive, so the command retrieves all the items in the C:\Data directory.

A path beginning with a slash identifies a path from the root of the current drive. For example, if your current working location is C:\Scripts\PowerShell, the root of your drive is C. Therefore, the following command lists all items in the C:\Data directory:

```
Get-ChildItem \Data
```

If you do not specify a path beginning with a drive name, slash, or period when supplying the name of a container or item, the container or item is assumed to be located in the current working location. For example, if your current working location is C:\Scripts, the following command returns all the items in the C:\Scripts\PowerShell directory:

```
Get-ChildItem PowerShell
```

If you specify a file name rather than a directory name, PowerShell returns details about that file, as long as the file is available in the current working location. If the file is not available, PowerShell returns an error.

Chapter 5. Using Modules

Windows PowerShell modules are self-contained, reusable units of execution that can include:

- Script functions that are made available through .PSM1 files.
- .NET assemblies that are compiled into .DLL files and made available through .PSD1 files.
- PowerShell snap-ins that are made available in .DLL files.
- Custom views and data types that are described in .PS1XML files.

Module Essentials

Most modules have related snap-ins, .NET assemblies, custom views, and custom data types. In the .PSD1 files that define the included assemblies, you'll find an associative array that defines the properties of the module, as is shown in the example that follows and summarized in Table 5-1.

```
@{
    GUID = '41486F7D-842F-40F1-ACE4-8405F9C2ED9B'
    Author="Microsoft Corporation"
    CompanyName="Microsoft Corporation"
    Copyright="© Microsoft Corporation. All rights
reserved."
    ModuleVersion = '2.0.0.0'
    PowerShellVersion = '3.0'
    FormatsToProcess = 'Storage.format.ps1xml'
    TypesToProcess = 'Storage.types.ps1xml'
    NestedModules = @('Disk.cdxml', 'DiskImage.cdxml',
'Partition.cdxml', 'VirtualDisk.cdxml',
'PhysicalDisk.cdxml', 'StorageEnclosure.cdxml',
'StorageNode.cdxml', 'StoragePool.cdxml',
'ResiliencySetting.cdxml', 'StorageProvider.cdxml',
'StorageSubSystem.cdxml', 'Volume.cdxml',
'StorageSetting.cdxml',
```

```
'MaskingSet.cdxml','InitiatorId.cdxml','InitiatorPort.cdxml'
,'TargetPort.cdxml','TargetPortal.cdxml','StorageCmdlets.cdx
ml', 'OffloadDataTransferSetting.cdxml', 'StorageJob.cdxml',
'StorageTier.cdxml', 'FileIntegrity.cdxml',
'StorageReliabilityCounter.cdxml', 'FileStorageTier.cdxml' )
```

TABLE 5-1 Common Properties of Modules

PROPERTY	DESCRIPTION
Author, CompanyName, Copyright	Provides information about the creator of the module and copyright.
CLRVersion	The common language runtime (CLR) version of the .NET Framework required by the module.
CmdletsToExport	Cmdlets the module supports.
Description	The descriptive name of the module.
FormatsToProcess	A list of FORMAT.PS1XML files loaded by the module to create custom views for the module's cmdlets.
GUID	The globally unique identifier (GUID) of the module.
ModuleVersion	The version and revision number of the module.
NestedModules	A list of snap-ins, .NET assemblies, or both loaded by the module.

PowerShellVersion	The version of PowerShell required by the module. The version specified or a later version must be installed for the module to work.
RequiredAssemblies	A list of .NET assemblies that must be loaded for the module to work.
TypesToProcess	A list of TYPES.PS1XML files loaded by the module to create custom data types for the module's cmdlets.

Working with Modules

Although PowerShell includes a New-Module cmdlet for creating dynamic modules from script blocks, you'll more commonly use Get-Module, Import-Module, and Remove-Module to work with existing modules. You can list the available modules by entering **get-module -listavailable**. However, this will give you the full definition of each module in list format. A better way to find available modules is to look for them by name, path, and description:

```
get-module -listavailable | format-list name, path,
description
```

You can also look for them only by name and description:

```
get-module -listavailable | format-table name, description
```

If you want to determine the availability of a specific module, enter the following command:

```
get-module -listavailable [-name] ModuleNames
```

where ModuleNames is a comma-separated list of modules to check. You can enter module names with or without the associated file extension and use wildcards such as. Note that when you use the –ListAvailable parameter, the
–Name parameter is position sensitive, allowing you to specify modules using either

```
get-module -listavailable -name ModuleNames
```

or

```
get-module -listavailable ModuleNames
```

Here is an example:

```
get-module -listavailable -name networkloadbalancingclusters
```

Obtaining and Installing Modules

The core set of modules available in PowerShell depends on the versions of Windows you are running as well as the components that are installed. The components for available modules are registered in the operating system as necessary but are not added to your PowerShell sessions by default (in most instances). Additionally, modules that define functions and include .PSM1 files require an execution policy to be set so that signed scripts can run.

Only installed modules are available for use. Windows and Windows Server include some pre-installed modules. Most other modules are installed as part of system configuration. For example, when you add roles or features in Server Manager, Server Manager installs any PowerShell modules related to these roles or features. Installing the Remote Server Administration Tools feature on your management computer also will install the PowerShell modules for tools you select for installation.

You don't necessarily need to install modules on your management computer to use them. When you connect to a remote computer from your management computer, modules installed on the remote computer typically are implicitly imported into the session. This allows you to use the modules to manage the remote computer.

> **NOTE**   If your organization has in-house developed modules, you may want to install modules on particular computers to work with these modules. Here, modules typically are stored in folders and you can copy these folders from one computer to another to install a module. The key is to ensure you copy the folder and its contents to a location specified by the $env:PSModulePath variable. $env:PSModulePath determines the path that PowerShell searches for modules.

Importing Modules

Beginning with PowerShell 3.0, installed modules are imported automatically the first time you use a command in a module. Because of this, you don't need to explicitly import modules as was required previously. For example, PowerShell imports the Micrsoft.PowerShell.Utility module when you run the Get-Alias cmdlet, making all the cmdlets in this module available without having to import the module again.

Modules are also imported:

- When you get help for a command using Get-Help.

- When you get a command using Get-Command.

Because the wildcard character (*) performs a search rather than actual use of a command, modules are not imported when you use * with Get-Help and Get-Command. Other important caveats to keep in mind:

- Only modules stored in the location specified by $env:PSModulePath are imported automatically. Modules in other locations are not imported automatically.
- Only modules delivered as folders are imported automatically. Modules that consist of a file, such as a .DLL or .PSM1 file, are not imported automatically.
- Commands that use providers may not cause the related module to be imported. If so, the provider won't be available.
- The $PSModuleAutoloadingPreference variable can be configured to enable, disable and configure automatic importing of modules. If automatic importing of modules is disabled, you must always explicitly import modules.

You can explicitly import an available module into the current session by using the Import-Module cmdlet. The basic syntax is to follow Import-Module with the name of the module to import. For example, to import the WebAdminstration module, type **import-module webadministration**. After you import a module, its providers, cmdlets, functions and other features are available in the console session.

> **NOTE** There are several reasons for explicitly importing modules rather than having PowerShell implicitly import modules. One reason is simply to ensure the module you want to work with is available in the current session. Also, if you want to ensure a module's commands don't replace existing commands, you may

> want to use the –Prefix or –NoClobber parameters of Import-Module. The –Prefix parameters adds a unique prefix to the noun names of all imported commands. The –NoClobber parameter prevents the module from adding commands that would replace existing commands in the session.

If you add the necessary Import-Module commands to a relevant profile, you can be sure that modules you want to use are always loaded when available. To find imported modules or to verify that an additional module is imported, enter the following command:

```
get-module | format-table name, description
```

Any module listed in the output is imported and available.

To remove a module from the current session, use the Remove-Module cmdlet. The basic syntax is to follow Remove-Module with the name of the module to remove. For example, to remove the WebAdministration module from the current session, type **remove-module webadministration**. The module is still loaded, but the providers, cmdlets, and other features that it supports are no longer available.

You will often want to be sure that a particular module has been imported before you try to use its features. In the following example, when the WebAdministration module is available, the statement in parentheses evaluates to True, and any code in the related script block is executed:

```
if (get-module -name WebAdministration -erroraction
silentlycontinue)
  {

  Code to execute if the module is available.

} else {
```

```
Code to execute if the module is not available.
```

```
}
```

As shown previously, you could add an Else clause to define alternative actions. As before, I set the –ErrorAction parameter to SilentlyContinue so that error messages aren't written to the output if the module has not been imported.

Chapter 6. Enabling Remote Commands

Remote access in Windows PowerShell 3.0 and Windows PowerShell 4.0 is made available through:

- PowerShell sessions which use the PowerShell remoting features.
- Common Information Model (CIM) sessions which use PowerShell remoting features by default (but also can use DCOM).
- PowerShell Web Access which allows you to connect to a web gateway application running on IIS, which in turns executes your remote commands.

NOTE To work remotely, your computer and the remote computer must be properly configured. Individual cmdlets provide access to remote computers as well. Here, you use the –ComputerName parameter of these cmdlets, the cmdlets connect to the remote machine over Distributed COM (DCOM), and return the results to the local machine. For example, when you use the –ComputerName parameter of Get-Process to examine processes on remote computers, Get-Process communicates with the remote computers using DCOM and not the standard PowerShell remoting features. The exception is for session-related commands, as well as Invoke-Command, which always use either an implicitly created session or an explicitly created session. With sessions, PowerShell remoting works as discussed in this section.

REAL WORLD PowerShell Web Access is a feature of Windows Server 2012 and later. Although you'll hear that PowerShell Web Access allows you to connect to a remote computer through a web browser, technically, that isn't accurate. With PowerShell Web Access, you establish a connection to a remote server using the URI address of its HTTP or HTTPS endpoint. These connections are made over the standard TCP ports for web traffic, which by default are port 80 for HTTP and port 443 for HTTPS, but they are not established using a web browser.

Remoting Fundamentals

When you use the –ComputerName parameter of many cmdlets, the cmdlets connect to the remote machine over Distributed COM (DCOM). As DCOM uses RPC calls on dynamic ports, you may not be able to manage remote computers through firewalls. For example, when trying to work remotely through a firewall that isn't configured to allow DCOM traffic, you will get an "RPC server is not available" error and won't be able to connect. Although an administrator could configure a firewall to allow this traffic, this typically requires using a less secure configuration.

In contrast, the standard PowerShell remoting features use the WS-Management (WSMan) protocol and the Windows Remote Management (WinRM) service. When you use WSMan, PowerShell remoting connects your local PowerShell session with a PowerShell session on a remote computer. Commands you enter in the local session are sent to the remote computer, executed locally on the remote computer, and then the results are returned to your local PowerShell session. As everything runs within the same framework, you can be certain that you can consistently work with remote computers as long as you know how to establish remote sessions using PowerShell.

PowerShell remoting has significant advantages over using standard applications for remote management. One advantage is that a single TCP port is used for all standard communications and a single TCP port is used for all secure communications, which by default are ports 5985 and 5986 respectively. Thus, when you are connecting to remote computers through firewalls, only these TCP ports need to be open to establish connections.

Another significant advantage is that from a single console you can simultaneously work with multiple remote computers. To do this, you simply establish a session with the computers you want to work with and then execute commands within the context of that session.

Configuring Remoting

WinRM must be configured appropriately on any computer that you want to manage remotely. You can verify the availability of WinRM and configure PowerShell for remoting via WinRM by following these steps:

1. Start Windows PowerShell as an administrator by right-clicking the Windows PowerShell shortcut and selecting Run As Administrator.

2. The WinRM service is configured for manual startup by default. You must change the startup type to Automatic and start the service on each computer you want to work with. At the PowerShell prompt, you can verify that the WinRM service is running using the following command:

```
get-service winrm
```

As shown in the following example, the value of the Status property in the output should be Running:

```
Status     Name                DisplayName
------     ----                -----------
Running    WinRM               Windows Remote Management
```

3. To configure Windows PowerShell for remoting via WinRM, type the following command:

```
Enable-PSRemoting -force
```

You can use Test-WsMan to verify that a remote computer is configured correctly and determine the version of WSMan available.

Connecting Between Domains and in Workgroups

In many cases, you will be able to work with remote computers in other domains. However, if the remote computer is not in a trusted domain, the remote computer might not be able to authenticate your credentials. To enable authentication, you need to add the remote computer to the list of trusted hosts for the local computer in WinRM.

You have several options for modifying the list of trusted hosts. The first option is to use the WinRM command-line utility and replace the existing list of trusted hosts with the value you specify using the following syntax

```
winrm s winrm/config/client
'@{TrustedHosts="RemoteComputer"}'
```

where RemoteComputer is the name or IP address of the remote computer, such as

```
winrm s winrm/config/client '@{TrustedHosts="CorpServer56"}'
```

Or

```
winrm s winrm/config/client
'@{TrustedHosts="192.168.10.80"}'
```

To confirm that the computer was added to the TrustHosts list, display the WinRM client configuration details by entering: **winrm g winrm/config/client**.

Another way to specify a remote host to trust is to use Set-Item and the WSMan: provider to modify the TrustedHosts list. Unlike the WinRM utility, which replaces the trusted hosts list, the WSMan: provider adds the value you specify to the existing list, making it easier for you to specify multiple trusted hosts. The basic syntax is:

```
Set-Item -Path WSMan:\localhost\Client\TrustedHosts
-Value 'RemoteComputer'
```

where RemoteComputer is the name of the remote computer, such as

```
Set-Item -Path WSMan:\localhost\Client\TrustedHosts
-Value 'MailServer12'
```

NOTE Typically, you are prompted to confirm that you want to modify the TrustedHosts lists. Confirm that you do by pressing Y. To bypass this message, use the –Force parameter. Note also that you can set values in this way because the WSMan: provider adds the value to the existing value by setting –Concatenate to $true automatically.

If you're wondering which hosts are trusted, you can list trusted hosts by entering:

```
Get-Item -Path WSMan:\localhost\Client\TrustedHosts |fl
name, value
```

When you are working with computers in workgroups, accessing a domain computer from a workgroup or vice versa, you must either use HTTPS as the transport or add the remote machine to the TrustedHosts configuration settings. If you cannot connect to a remote host, verify that the service on the remote host is running and is accepting requests by running the following command on the remote host:

```
winrm quickconfig
```

This command analyzes and configures the WinRM service. If the WinRM service is set up correctly, you'll see output similar to the following:

```
WinRM service is already running on this machine.
WinRM is already set up for remote management on this
computer.
```

If the WinRM service is not set up correctly, you see output similar to the following and need to respond affirmatively to several prompts. When this process completes, WinRM should be set up correctly.

```
WinRM Quick Configuration
Running command "Set-WSManQuickConfig" to enable remote
management of this computer by using the Windows Remote
Management (WinRM) service.
 This includes:
1. Starting or restarting (if already started) the WinRM
service
2. Setting the WinRM service startup type to Automatic
3. Creating a listener to accept requests on any IP address
4. Enabling Windows Firewall inbound rule exceptions for WS-
Management traffic (for http only).

Do you want to continue?
[Y] Yes   [A] Yes to All   [N] No   [L] No to All   [S] Suspend
[?] Help (default is "Y"): Y
WinRM has been updated to receive requests.
WinRM service type changed successfully.

WinRM has been updated for remote management.
Created a WinRM listener on HTTP://* to accept WS-Man
requests to any IP on this machine.
WinRM firewall exception enabled.
```

```
Confirm
Are you sure you want to perform this action?
Performing the operation "Set-PSSessionConfiguration" on
target "Name: microsoft.powershell SDDL:
O:NSG:BAD:P(A;;GA;;;BA)(A;;GA;;;RM)S:P(AU;FA;GA;;;WD)(AU;SA;
GXGW;;;WD). This lets selected users remotely run Windows
PowerShell commands on this computer.".
[Y] Yes   [A] Yes to All   [N] No   [L] No to All   [S] Suspend
[?] Help (default is "Y"): Y
```

Creating HTTPS and Other Listeners

By default, WinRM QuickConfig creates an HTTP listener on a remote host, but does not create an HTTPS listener. If you want to make HTTPS connections to the remote host, you'll do the following:

1. Obtain an SSL certificate for the remote computer and make sure the certificate has common name (CN) entry that matches the identifier you are using.

2. Install the remote computer's SSL certificate in the certificate store for the management computer you are using (and not the user's certificate store).

3. On the remote computer, use New-WSManInstance to add an HTTPS listener for WSMan.

To create an HTTPS listener for WSMan, you need the thumbprint value of the remote computer's SSL certificate. One way to obtain this value is to access the Cert: provider and list the certificate thumbprints, as shown in this example:

```
Get-ChildItem -Path cert:\LocalMachine -Recurse |
select Subject, FriendlyName, Thumbprint | fl
```

After you obtain the certificate thumbprint, you can use New-WSManInstance to create the HTTPS listener on the remote computer, such as:

```
$thumbprint = "XXX-XXXX-XX-XXXX-XX"
New-WSManInstance -ResourceURI winrm/config/Listener
-SelectorSet @{Transport='HTTPS',
Address="IP:192.168.10.34"}
-ValueSet @{Hostname="Server12.Imaginedlands.com",
CertificateThumbprint=$thumprint}
```

Here, you create an HTTPS listener for Server12. As mentioned previously, WinRM listens on port 5985 for HTTP and port 5986 for HTTPS. Although you can configure alternate listening ports, you must delete the current listening port before creating a new listening port, as shown in this example:

```
winrm delete winrm/config/listener?Address=*+Transport=HTTP
```

```
winrm create winrm/config/listener?Address=*+Transport=HTTP
@{Port="5999"}
```

> **NOTE** As the port change applies to all computers and sessions the computer runs, you should only change the listening port if required by IT policy or firewall settings.

Generally, to use PowerShell remoting features, you must start Windows PowerShell as an administrator by right-clicking the Windows PowerShell shortcut and selecting Run As Administrator. When starting PowerShell from another program, such as the command prompt (cmd.exe), you must start that program as an administrator.

Chapter 7. Executing Remote Commands

You can use Windows PowerShell remoting to run cmdlets and external programs on remote computers. For example, you can run any built-in cmdlets and external programs accessible in the PATH environment variable ($env:path). However, because PowerShell runs as a network service or local service, you cannot use PowerShell to open the user interface for any program on a remote computer. If you try to start a program with a graphical interface, the program process starts but the command cannot complete, and the PowerShell prompt does not return until the program is finished or you press Ctrl+C.

Understanding Remote Execution

When you submit a remote command, the command is transmitted across the network to the Windows PowerShell client on the designated remote computer, and runs in the Windows PowerShell client on the remote computer. The command results are sent back to the local computer and appear in the Windows PowerShell session on the local computer. Note that all of the local input to a remote command is collected before being sent to the remote computer, but the output is returned to the local computer as it is generated.

Whenever you use PowerShell remoting features, keep the following in mind:

- You must start Windows PowerShell as an administrator by right-clicking the Windows PowerShell shortcut and selecting Run As Administrator. When starting PowerShell from another program, such as the command prompt (cmd.exe), you must start that program as an administrator.

- The current user must be a member of the Administrators group on the remote computer or be able to provide the credentials of an administrator. When you connect to a remote computer, PowerShell uses your user name and password credentials to log on to the remote computer. The credentials are encrypted.

- When you work remotely, you use multiple instances of Windows PowerShell: a local instance and one or more remote instances. Generally, in the local instance, the policies and profiles on the local computer are in effect. On a remote instance, the policies and profiles on the remote computer are in effect. This means cmdlets, aliases, functions, preferences, and other elements in the local profile are not necessarily available to remote commands. To ensure you can use cmdlets, aliases, functions, preferences, and other elements in the local profile with remote commands, you must copy the local profiles to each remote computer.

- Although you can execute commands on remote computers, any files, directories, and additional resources that are needed to execute a command must exist on the remote computer. Additionally, your user account must have permission to connect to the remote computer, permission to run Windows PowerShell, and permission to access files, directories, and other resources on the remote computer.

- The functionality available through your remote session depends on the version of PowerShell on the remote computer. For example, if you connect to a remote computer that has PowerShell 3.0 installed, you cannot use the features of PowerShell 4.0, even if PowerShell 4.0 is available on your local machine.

Standard Commands for Remoting

Except when you are using CIM sessions, the cmdlets you'll use for remoting include:

- **Connect-PSSession**   Reconnects to one or more PowerShell sessions that were disconnected. You can use Connect-PSSession to connect to any valid disconnected session, including those that were started in other sessions or on other computers, those that were disconnected intentionally, such as by using the Disconnect-PSSession cmdlet, and that were disconnected unintentionally, such as by a network interruption when running the Invoke-Command cmdlet. Session objects are instantiated when you create a session in the PowerShell console or the PowerShell application. A session object is created for each remote computer to which you connect. As long as the session objects are valid and you have appropriate credentials, you can use these objects to reconnect to the sessions.
- **Disconnect-PSSession**   Disconnects a PowerShell session. You can only disconnect from open non-interactive sessions, meaning you can disconnect from sessions started with New-PSSession but cannot disconnect from sessions started with Enter-PSSession. Additionally, you cannot disconnect from closed or broken sessions.
- **Enter-PSSession**   Starts an interactive session with a single remote computer. During the session, you can run commands just as if you were typing directly on the remote computer. You can have only one interactive session at a time. Typically, you use the –ComputerName parameter to specify the name of the remote computer. However, you can also use a session that you created previously by using New-PSSession for the interactive session.

- **Exit-PSSession** Ends an interactive session and disconnects from the remote computer. You can also type **exit** to end an interactive session. The effect is the same as using Exit-PSSession.
- **Export-PSSession** Gets cmdlets, functions, aliases, and other command types from an open session and saves them in a Windows PowerShell script module file (.psm1). When you want to use the commands from the script module, use the Add-Module cmdlet to add the commands to the local session so that they can be used. To export commands, first use New-PSSession to connect to the session that has the commands that you want to export. Then use Export-PSSession to export the commands. By default, Export-PSSession exports all commands except for commands that already exist in the session. However, you can use the –PSSnapin, –CommandName, and –CommandType parameters to specify the commands to export.
- **Get-PSSession** Gets the PowerShell sessions (PSSessions) that were created in the current session. Without parameters, this cmdlet returns all available PSSessions. You can use the parameters of Get-PSSession to get the sessions that are connected to particular computers or identify sessions by their names, IDs, or instance IDs. For computers, type the NetBIOS name, IP address, or fully qualified domain name. To specify the local computer, enter the computer name, localhost, or a dot (.). For IDs, type an integer value that uniquely identifies the PSSession in the current session. PSSessions can be assigned friendly names with the –Name parameter. You can reference the friendly names using wildcards. To find the names and IDs of PSSessions, use Get-PSSession without parameters. An instance ID is a GUID that uniquely identifies a PSSession, even when you have multiple sessions running in PowerShell. The instance ID is stored in the RemoteRunspaceID property of the RemoteRunspaceInfo object that represents a PSSession. To find the InstanceID of the PSSessions

in the current session, enter **get-pssession | Format-Table Name, ComputerName, RemoteRunspaceId**.

- **Import-PSSession** Imports cmdlets, aliases, functions, and other command types from an open session into the current session on your management computer. You can import any command that Get-Command can find in the other session. To import commands, first use New-PSSession to connect to the session from which you will import. Then use Import-PSSession to import commands. By default, Import-PSSession imports all commands except for commands that exist in the current session. To overwrite existing commands, use the –AllowClobber parameter. PowerShell adds the imported commands to a temporary module that exists only in your session, and it returns an object that represents the module. Although you can use imported commands just as you would use any command in the session, the imported part of the command actually runs in the session from which it was imported. Because imported commands might take longer to run than local commands, Import-PSSession adds an –AsJob parameter to every imported command. This parameter allows you to run the command as a PowerShell background job.

- **Invoke-Command** Runs commands on a local computer or one or more remote computers, and returns all output from the commands, including errors. Use the –ComputerName parameter to run a single command on a remote computer. To run a series of related commands that share data, create a PowerShell session (PSSession) on a remote computer, and then use the –Session parameter of Invoke-Command to run the command in the PSSession or use the –InDisconnectedSession parameter to run commands without maintaining persistent connections to the remote sessions.

- **New-PSSession** Creates a PowerShell session (PSSession) on a local or remote computer. When you create a PSSession, Windows

PowerShell establishes a persistent connection to the remote computer, and you can use the PSSession to interact directly with the computer.

- **Receive-PSSession**   Gets the results of commands running in PowerShell sessions that were disconnected. Receive-PSSession connects to the session, resumes any commands that were suspended, and gets the results of commands running in the session. You can use a Receive-PSSession in addition to or in place of a Connect-PSSession command. Receive-PSSession can connect to any disconnected or reconnected session, including those that were started in other sessions or on other computers, those that were disconnected intentionally, such as by using the Disconnect-PSSession cmdlet, and that were disconnected unintentionally, such as by a network interruption when running the Invoke-Command cmdlet. If you use the Receive-PSSession cmdlet to connect to a session in which no commands are running or suspended, Receive-PSSession connects to the session, but returns no output or errors.
- **Remove-PSSession**   Closes one or more PowerShell sessions and frees the resources the sessions were using. It is a best practice to remove sessions when you are finished using them.

Invoking Remote Commands

One way to run commands on remote computers is to use the Invoke-Command cmdlet. With this cmdlet, you can do the following:

- Run commands in an implicitly-created PowerShell session, in an explicitly-created PowerShell session, in a disconnected session, or as a background job.

- Use the –ComputerName parameter to specify the remote computers to work with by DNS name, NetBIOS name, or IP address.
- When working with multiple remote computers, separate each computer name or IP address with a comma.
- Enclose your command or commands to execute in curly braces, which denotes a script block, and use the –ScriptBlock parameter to specify the command or commands to run.

For example, you can type the following command as a single line to run a Get-Process command remotely:

```
invoke-command -computername Server43, Server27, Server82
-scriptblock {get-process}
```

Here, you are opening temporary sessions to Server43, Server27 and Server82, and running the Get-Process command. The results from the command execution on each remote computer are returned as results to the local computer. If the temporary session is interrupted, such as by a network or power outage, PowerShell creates a background job for the disconnected session, which makes it easier to reconnect, resume execution and get the results.

> **MORE INFO**   Although you are using an implicitly created session, the session works much like a standard PowerShell session. As discussed in "Understanding Remote Execution and Object Serialization," this means PowerShell connects over WSMan, the results are serialized using XML, and passed over WSMan back to the local machine where the results are deserialized.
>
> By default, Invoke-Command runs under your user name and credentials. Use the –Credential parameter to specify alternate credentials using the UserName or Domain\UserName syntax. You will be prompted for a password.

> **REAL WORLD**   When you connect to a remote computer that is running Windows or Windows Server, the default starting location is the home directory of the current user, which is stored in the %HomePath% environment variable ($env:homepath) and the Windows PowerShell $home variable.

When you use Invoke-Command, the cmdlet returns an object that includes the name of the computer that generated the data. The remote computer name is stored in the PSComputerName property. Typically, the PSComputerName property is displayed by default. You can use the – HideComputerName parameter to hide the PSComputerName property.

If the PSComputerName property isn't displayed and you want to see the source computer name, use the Format-Table cmdlet to add the PSComputerName property to the output as shown in the following example:

```
$procs = invoke-command -script {get-process | sort-object
-property Name} -computername Server56, Server42, Server27

&$procs | format-table Name, Handles, WS, CPU,
PSComputerName -auto
```

Name	Handles	WS	CPU	PSComputerName
acrotray	52	3948544	0	Server56
AlertService	139	7532544		Server56
csrss	594	20463616		Server56
csrss	655	5283840		Server56
CtHelper	96	6705152	0.078125	Server56
acrotray	43	3948234	0	Server42
AlertService	136	7532244		Server42
csrss	528	20463755		Server42
csrss	644	5283567		Server42

CtHelper	95	6705576	0.067885 Server42
acrotray	55	3967544	0 Server27
AlertService	141	7566662	Server27
csrss	590	20434342	Server27
csrss	654	5242340	Server27
CtHelper	92	6705231	0.055522 Server27

> **NOTE**   It's important to point out that because the object is serialized and deserialized, the object's methods aren't available. Although this happens across any WSMan connection, this doesn't happen when DCOM is used.

PowerShell includes a per-command throttling feature that lets you limit the number of concurrent remote connections that are established for a command. Generally, the default is 32 or 50 concurrent connections, depending on the cmdlet. You can use the –ThrottleLimit parameter to set a custom throttle limit for a command. Keep in mind the throttling feature is applied to each command, not to the entire session or to the computer. If you are running a command concurrently in several sessions, the number of concurrent connections is the sum of the concurrent connections in all sessions.

Keep in mind that although PowerShell can manage hundreds of concurrent remote connections, the number of remote commands that you can send might be limited by the resources of your computer and its ability to establish and maintain multiple network connections. To add more protection for remoting, you can use the –UseSSL parameter of Invoke-Command. As with commands that are run locally, you can pause or terminate a remote command by pressing Ctrl+S or Ctrl+C.

> **REAL WORLD**   PowerShell remoting is available even when the local computer is not in a domain. For testing and development, you

can use the remoting features to connect to and create sessions on the same computer. PowerShell remoting works the same as when you are connecting to a remote computer.

To run remote commands on a computer in a workgroup, you might need to change Windows security settings on the management and target computers. On the target computer, meaning to which you want to connect, you must allow remote access to the computer using Enable-PSRemoting –Force. On your management computer, meaning the computer you are working from, you must either run Enable-PSRemoting or do the following: ensure the WinRM service is started and enable the local account token filter policy by ensuring the LocalAccountTokenFilterPolicy registry entry in HKLM\SOFTWARE\Microsoft\Windows\CurrentVersion\Policies\System has its value set to 1.

You can determine whether the WinRM service is running by entering **Get-Service WinRM**. You can check the version of WinRM that's installed by entering **Test-WSMan –Auth default**. Enter **Get-PSSessionConfiguration** to check the remoting configuration for PowerShell.

Chapter 8. Establishing PowerShell Sessions

Windows PowerShell supports both local and remote sessions. A *session* is a runspace that establishes a common working environment for commands. Commands in a session can share data. After you create a session, you can work with it interactively by using Enter-PSSession or you can invoke commands against the session by using Invoke-Command. When you are finished using a session, you can disconnect from it and reconnect later or you can exit the session to free up the resources used by the session.

Invoking Sessions

Using the New-PSSession cmdlet, you can establish a session to create a persistent connection to a computer you want to work with. Unless you use the –ComputerName parameter and use it to specify the name of one or more remote computers, PowerShell assumes you are creating a session for the local computer. With New-PSSession, you must use the –Session parameter with Invoke-Command to run the command in the named session. For example, you can establish a session by typing the following command:

```
$s = New-PSSession -ComputerName Server24
```

Here, *$s* is a variable that stores the session object. PowerShell knows you are creating a remote session because you've used the –ComputerName parameter. PowerShell creates a persistent connection with the specified computer. Use Invoke-Command with the –Session parameter to run the command in the named session as shown in this example:

```
invoke-command -session $s -scriptblock {get-process}
```

Here, you use Invoke-Command to run Get-Process in the $s session. Because this session is connected to a remote computer, the command runs on the remote computer.

When you create a session, you can control the session via the session object that is returned. If you want to get information about remote sessions on a particular remote computer, you can use Get-PSSession. For example, you could enter **get-pssession –ComputerName Server24 | fl**. You'd then see detailed information about remote sessions on this computer and their status, such as:

```
ComputerName            : CorpServer134
ConfigurationName       : Microsoft.PowerShell
InstanceId              :
Id                      : 2
Name                    : IT
Availability            : Available
ApplicationPrivateData  : {DebugMode, DebugStop,
PSVersionTable, DebugBreakpointCount}
Runspace                :
System.Management.Automation.RemoteRunspace
State                   : Opened
IdleTimeout             : 7200000
OutputBufferingMode     : Block
DisconnectedOn          :
ExpiresOn               :
```

As you can see from the output, the session is assigned the session ID of 2. This ID also can be used to work with or get information about the session. For example, if you enter **get-pssession –id 2 | fl** you'd get the same information.

> **NOTE** Sessions also can be controlled via a name assigned when invoking the session. Use the –Name parameter to set the name. If you don't specify a name for the session, a default name typically is assigned, based on the ID of the session. For example, if the session ID is 11, the automatically assigned name typically is Session11.

The output of Get-PSSession provides additional information that is useful for working with sessions, including:

- **ConfigurationName** Specifies the type of session, which is important for differentiating PowerShell sessions and CIM sessions. PowerShell sessions are listed as Microsoft.PowerShell.
- **Availability** Specifies the availability of the session with respect to the current PowerShell window. A session listed as Available was created in the current window. A session listed with another value wasn't created in the current window. Generally, None means the session is not available and Busy means the session is active in another window or on another computer.
- **State** Specifies the state of the session. A session listed as Opened was created in the current window and is active. A session listed as Broken was unintentionally disconnected. A session listed as Disconnected was intentionally disconnected.

Although the examples so far work with one computer, you can just as easily establish a session with multiple computers. Simply establish the session and name all the computers in a comma-separated list, such as:

```
$s = New-PSSession -ComputerName Server24, Server37,
Server92
```

By default, your current credentials are used to establish connections. However, you might also need to specify a user account that has permissions to perform remote administration using the –Credential parameter.

You can provide alternative credentials in one of two ways. You can:

- Pass in a Credential object to provide the information required for authentication. A Credential object has UserName and Password properties. Although the user name is stored as a regular string, the password is stored as a secure, encrypted string.
- Specify the user account that has permission to perform the action. After you specify a user name, PowerShell displays a prompt for the user's password. When prompted, enter the password and then click OK.

> **REAL WORLD**   With credentials, the user name can be provided in several formats. If you are working in a domain and the appropriate domain is already shown in the credentials dialog box, you don't have to specify the domain as part of the user name. However, if you are working in a domain and the domain isn't set, you should provide the required domain and user information using the Domain\UserName format, such as ImaginedL\WilliamS for the user WilliamS working in the ImaginedL domain. Additionally, if you want to work with a local computer account rather than a domain account, you can specify a local computer account using the ComputerName\UserName format, such as PC29\TomG for the local user TomG on PC29.

To see how the –Credential parameter can be used, consider the following example:

```
$t = New-PSSession -ComputerName Server24, Server45,
Server36 -Credential Cpandl\WilliamS
```

Here, you establish a session with Server24, Server45, and Server36 and specify your domain and user name. As a result, when you use Invoke-Command to run commands in the $t session, the commands run on each remote computer with those credentials. Note that although this is a single session, each runspace on each computer is separate.

Extending this idea, you can also just as easily get the list of remote computers from a text file. In this example, servers.txt contains a comma-separated list of computers:

```
$ses = get-content c:\test\servers.txt | new-pssession
-credential cpandl\williams
```

Here, the contents of the Servers.txt file are piped to New-PSSession. As a result, the $ses session is established with all computers listed in the file. Typically, the names are provided in a comma-separate list, such as:

```
Server14, Server87, Server21
```

Sometimes, you'll want to execute an application or external utility on a remote computer as shown in the following example:

```
$comp = get-content c:\computers.txt
$s = new-pssession -computername $comp
invoke-command -session $s { powercfg.exe -energy }
```

Here, C:\Computers.txt is the path to the file containing the list of remote computers to check. On each computer, you run PowerCfg with the –Energy parameter. This generates an Energy-Report.html file in the default directory for the user account used to access the computer. The energy report provides details on power configuration settings and issues that are causing power management not to work correctly. If you'd rather not have to retrieve the report from each computer, you can write the report to a share and base the report name on the computer name, as shown in the following example:

```
$comp = get-content c:\computers.txt
$s = new-pssession -computername $comp

invoke-command -session $s { powercfg.exe -energy -output
"\\fileserver72\reports\$env:computername.html"}
```

Here, you write the report to the \\fileserver72\reports share and name the file using the value of the ComputerName environment variable. Note that when you work with PowerShell and are referencing applications and external utilities, you must specify the .exe file extension with the program name.

When you are running commands on many remote computers, you might not want to wait for the commands to return before performing other tasks. To avoid having to wait, use Invoke-Command with the –AsJob parameter to create a background job in each of the runspaces:

```
invoke-command –session $s -scriptblock {get-process moddr |
stop-process -force } -AsJob
```

Here, you use Invoke-Command to get and stop a named process via the $s session. Because the command is run as a background job, the prompt returns immediately without waiting for the command to run on each computer.

Although being able to establish a session on many computers is handy, sometimes you might want to work interactively with a single remote computer. To do this, you can use the Enter-PSSession cmdlet to start an interactive session with a remote computer. At the Windows Powershell prompt, type **Enter-PSSession *ComputerName***, where *ComputerName* is the name of the remote computer. The command prompt changes to show that you are connected to the remote computer, as shown in the following example:

```
[Server49]: PS C:\Users\wrstanek.cpandl\Documents>
```

Now the commands that you type run on the remote computer just as if you had typed them directly on the remote computer. For enhanced security through encryption of transmissions, the Enter-PSSession cmdlet also supports the –Credential and –UseSSL parameters. You can end the interactive session using the command Exit-PSSession or by typing **exit**.

Understanding Remote Execution and Object Serialization

When you are working with remote computers, you need to keep in mind the following:

- How commands are executed
- How objects are serialized

Whether you use Invoke-Command or Enter-PSSession with remote computers, Windows PowerShell establishes a temporary connection, uses the connection to run the current command, and then closes the connection each time you run a command. This is an efficient method for running a single command or several unrelated commands, even on a large number of remote computers.

The New-PSSession cmdlet provides an alternative by establishing a session with a persistent connection. With New-PSSession, Windows PowerShell establishes a persistent connection and uses the connection to run any commands you enter. Because you can run multiple commands in a single, persistent runspace, the commands can share data, including the values of variables, the definitions of aliases, and the contents of functions. New-PSSession also supports the –UseSSL parameter.

When you use Windows PowerShell locally, you work with live .NET Framework objects, and these objects are associated with actual programs or components. When you invoke the methods or change the properties of live objects, the changes affect the actual program or component. And, when the properties of a program or component change, the properties of the object that represent them change too.

Because live objects cannot be transmitted over the network, Windows PowerShell serializes the objects sent in remote commands. This means it converts each object into a series of Constraint Language in XML (CLiXML) data elements for transmission. When Windows PowerShell receives a serialized file, it converts the XML into a deserialized object type. Although the deserialized object is an accurate record of the properties of the program or component at execution time, it is no longer directly associated with the originating component, and the methods are removed because they are no longer effective. Also, the serialized objects returned by the Invoke-Command cmdlet have additional properties that help you determine the origin of the command.

> **NOTE** You can use Export-Clixml to create XML-based representations of objects and store them in a file. The objects stored in the file are serialized. To import a CLiXML file and create deserialized objects, you can use Import-CLixml.

Disconnecting Sessions

With PowerShell 3.0 and later, sessions can be disconnected and reconnected. Although a power loss or temporary network outage can unintentionally disconnect you from a session, you disconnect from a session intentionally by using Disconnect-PSSession. Alternatively, you can run Invoke-Command with the –InDisconnectedSession parameter to run commands in a disconnected state.

When you disconnect from a session, any command or scripts that are running in the session continue running, and you can later reconnect to the session to pick up where you left off. You also can reconnect to a session if you were disconnected unintentionally.

Because you can only disconnect from open non-interactive sessions, you can disconnect from sessions started with New-PSSession, but cannot disconnect from sessions started with Enter-PSSession. Also, you cannot disconnect from closed or broken sessions, or sessions started in other PowerShell windows or by other users.

You can disconnect a session using its object, its ID or its name. In the following example, you create a session, work with the remote computer and then disconnect from the session:

```
$s = new-pssession -computername corpserver74
invoke-command -session $s { get-process }


. . .


disconnect-pssession -session $s
```

You can only disconnect sessions that are in the Opened state. To disconnect all open sessions at the same time, enter the following command:

```
Get-PSSession | Disconnect-PSSession
```

As you can't disconnect sessions that are already disconnected or broken, PowerShell will display errors if any sessions are in these states. To avoid these errors, you can use a filter to specify that you only want to disconnect Opened sessions. Here is an example:

```
get-pssession | where {$_.state -eq "Opened"} |
disconnect-pssession
```

Here, Get-PSSession lists all current sessions and then you filter the output using the Where-Object cmdlet so that only sessions with the State property set to Opened are passed through the pipeline and disconnected.

Sessions are considered to be idle when they are disconnected, even if commands are running. By default, sessions can be idle for 7200000 milliseconds (2 hours) before they are closed. Use –IdleTimeoutSec to specify a different timeout, up to 12 hours. In the following example, the time out is set to 8 hours (60 seconds x 60 x 8):

```
disconnect-pssession –session $s –idletimeout 60*60*8
```

> **REAL WORLD** The output buffering mode determines whether commands continue to run while a session is disconnected. The default output buffering mode for disconnected sessions is Block, which means command execution is suspended when the output buffer fills and doesn't resume again until the session is reconnected. Alternatively, you can set the output buffering mode

to Drop, which ensures that commands keep executing when the output buffer fills. However, with Drop, as new output is saved, the oldest output is discarded by default. To prevent this, redirect the command output to a file.

Reconnecting Sessions

To connect to any disconnected session, including those that were started in other sessions or on other computers, those that were disconnected intentionally, and those that were disconnected unintentionally, you have several choices. You can use either Connect-PSSession or Receive-PSSession.

The difference between connecting to a session and receiving a session is subtle but important. When you connect to a session, you reconnect to the session and are able to begin working with the remote computer or computers to which the session connects. When you receive a connection, you reconnect to the session, resume any commands that were suspended, and get the results of commands running in the session.

Whether you are reconnecting to a session using Connect-PSSession or Receive-PSSession, you need to identify the session to which you want to connect. If you are using the same computer and the same PowerShell window, you can enter **Get-PSSession** to list sessions by ID and name and then reconnect to sessions, as shown in the following examples:

```
connect-pssession -session $s
connect-pssession -id 2
connect-pssession -name CheckServerTasks
```

If you are using a different computer or PowerShell window, you'll need to use the –ComputerName parameter with Get-PSSession to list sessions on remote computers and then reconnect to sessions. Consider the following example and sample output:

```
Get-PSSession -ComputerName Server24, Server45, Server36
-Credential Cpandl\WilliamS

Id Name    ComputerName State ConfigurationName Availability
-- ----    ------------ ----- ----------------- ------------
2  Task    Server24 Disconnected Microsoft.PowerShell    None
3  Session12 Server45 Opened  Microsoft.PowerShell Available
4  Clnr    Server36 Broken        Microsoft.PowerShell    None
5  SChks   Server36 Disconnected Microsoft.PowerShell    Busy
```

Here, you find that each of the servers has active sessions. Although the session IDs are generated on a one up basis on the local computer, the session names are the actual names assigned either automatically or by users when the sessions were created. Note also that ComputerName identifies the remote computer and State specifies the state of the session as being Opened, Disconnected or Broken. Opened connections are already active in the current window.

You can reconnect disconnected and broken sessions, provided the sessions aren't active (busy). However, be sure to connect using the name assigned rather than the locally generated ID. For example, you could use the following command to reconnect to the Task session on Server24:

```
connect-pssession -computername server24 -name task
```

However, you could not use the locally generated session ID to connect to the Task session. Why? Because the session ID is locally generated and does not match the session ID on Server74.

PowerShell also allows you to reconnect multiple sessions simultaneously. Consider the following example and sample output:

```
Get-PSSession -ComputerName Server74, Server38, Server45
-Credential Cpandl\WilliamS
```

```
Id Name    ComputerName State   ConfigurationName Availability
-- ----    ------------ -----   ----------------- ------------
8  Session14 Server74   Disconnected Microsoft.PowerShell None
9  Session18 Server38   Broken       Microsoft.PowerShell None
10 SChks   Server45     Disconnected Microsoft.PowerShell None
```

Here, you have sessions on three different servers that are available to be connected. If you wanted to reconnect the sessions to continue working with the servers, the easiest way to do this would be to enter:

```
Get-PSSession -ComputerName Server74, Server38, Server45
-Credential Cpandl\WilliamS | Connect-PSSession
```

Or

```
$s = Get-PSSession -ComputerName Server74, Server38,
Server45 -Credential Cpandl\WilliamS | Connect-PSSession
```

Here, you get the sessions that were created on the remote computers and use Connect-PSSession to reconnect the sessions.

> **NOTE** Connect-PSSession has no effect on valid, active sessions. If the servers had sessions that were opened or disconnected but busy, those sessions would not be reconnected.

Once you've reconnected sessions, the sessions can be accessed in the current PowerShell window by ID and name. If you didn't assign the sessions to variables directly, you'll need to do so before you can work with the sessions using Invoke-Command. Enter **Get-PSSession** to get information about the sessions, and then use the (valid) locally assigned ID or the session name to assign sessions to a session variable, such as:

```
$session = get-pssession -id 2, 3, 12
```

Here, you store the session objects for the sessions with the local ID of 2, 3, and 12 in the $session variable. You can then use the $session variable to pass commands to all three remote computers, such as:

```
$session = get-pssession -id 2, 3, 12
```

```
invoke-command -session $session { get-eventlog system |
where {$_.entrytype -eq "Error"} }
```

When you are completely finished with a session, you should use Remove-PSSession to remove it. Removing a session stops any commands or scripts that are running, ends the session, and releases the resources the session was using.

Chapter 9. Connecting through PowerShell Web Access

PowerShell Web Access allows you to connect to a web gateway application running on IIS, which in turns executes your commands on a specified remote computer. The most commonly used implementation of PowerShell Web Access is with Exchange servers and Exchange Online.

With PowerShell Web Access, you establish connections to a remote computer using the URI address of the related HTTP or HTTPS endpoint. These connections are made over TCP port 80 for HTTP and TCP port 443 for HTTPS.

Before you can establish a connection to an HTTP or HTTPS endpoint and access PowerShell, you need to know:

- The configuration name, which is the naming context you want to use for working with the remote computer. For standard PowerShell, this is **Windows.PowerShell**. For Exchange server and Exchange Online, this is **Microsoft.Exchange**.
- The connection URI, which is the URL to PowerShell Web Access on the remote computer, such as http://server37.imaginedlands.com/PowerShell/.
- The authentication method to use. With Windows workgroups and domains, you typically use Kerberos authentication. With Exchange Online, you typically use Basic authentication.

When your management computer is joined to the domain in which you want to work, you can use either HTTP or HTTPS with Kerberos authentication to establish the PowerShell session. Keep in mind that with Kerberos authentication you must use the server name or the server's fully-qualified domain name and cannot use an IP address, as shown in the following example:

```
$Session = New-PSSession -ConfigurationName
Windows.PowerShell -ConnectionUri
http://Server24.imaginedlands.com/PowerShell/
-AllowRedirection -Authentication Kerberos
```

Here, you use the –AllowRedirection parameter to specify that redirection is allowed, which is required if the URI is redirected by the receiving server. You use HTTP with Kerberos authentication to connect to Server24. With Kerberos authentication, your current credentials are used to establish the session. If needed, you can pass in alternate credentials, as shown in this example:

```
$Cred = Get-Credential

$Session = New-PSSession -ConfigurationName
Windows.PowerShell -ConnectionUri
http://Server24.imaginedlands.com/PowerShell/
-AllowRedirection -Authentication Kerberos
-Credential $Cred
```

Here, when PowerShell executes Get-Credential, you are prompted for a user name and password. This credential is then stored in the $Cred variable. When PowerShell creates the remote session on Server24, the credential is passed in using the –Credential parameter.

If you want to use an authentication mechanism other than Kerberos or your computer isn't connected to the domain in which you want to work, you may need to use HTTPS as the transport (or the destination server must be added to the TrustedHosts configuration settings for WinRM, and HTTP must be enabled in the client configuration). You also must explicitly pass in a credential using the –Credential parameter, as shown in this example:

```
$Cred = Get-Credential

$Session = New-PSSession -ConfigurationName
Microsoft.Exchange -ConnectionUri
https://server17.imaginedlands.com/PowerShell/
-AllowRedirection -Authentication Negotiate
-Credential $Cred
```

> **REAL WORLD** Generally to work via HTTPS, the remote computer must have an SSL certificate. Regardless of whether you use Kerberos or another authentication mechanism, this certificate must contain a common name (CN) that matches the identifier you are using. You must install the remote computer's SSL certificate in the certificate store for the management computer you are using (and not the user's certificate store). Finally, you must ensure the remote computer has an HTTPS listener for WSMan. If you don't configure PowerShell in this way, you won't be able to connect using HTTPS.

After you establish a session with a remote server, you can import the server-side session into your client-side session by using the Import-PSSession cmdlet. The basic syntax is:

```
Import-PSSession [-Session] Session [-AllowClobber]
[-CommandType CommandTypes] [-Module Modules]
[-Prefix NounPrefix]
```

With Import-PSSession, you'll usually want to use the –AllowClobber parameter to specify that PowerShell can temporarily overwrite local commands, as shown in the following example:

```
Import-PSSession $Session -AllowClobber
```

Here, you import a session and overwrite local commands. By overwriting local commands, you ensure that any command you run is executed against the remote computer.

When you import a session, PowerShell creates an implicit remoting module and you no longer have to use Invoke-Command to execute commands on the remote computer. In this way, importing a PowerShell session by using Import-PSSession is similar to entering a session by using Enter-PSSession.

Temporarily overwriting commands is referred to as shadowing commands. As long as the remote session is valid, commands remain shadowed and are executed on the remote computer implicitly. If the connection is broken, however, commands won't execute on the remote machine as expected.

> **NOTE** When commands are shadowed, you can't use session-related commands to manage the session. Why? All commands are executed implicitly on the remote computer, which doesn't recognize the original session. To exit the session, you'll need to close the PowerShell window.

Keep in mind that if you don't use the –AllowClobber parameter, the import process won't temporarily overwrite local commands with those being imported from a remote session. As a result, you'll end up with a mixed environment where locally-defined commands execute against the local computer and imported commands execute against the remote computer. As this typically isn't what you want, you'll want to use –AllowClobber to ensure all commands are executed against the remote computer.

Chapter 10. Establishing CIM Sessions

Windows PowerShell 3.0 and later support the Common Information Model (CIM). CIM allows you to use XML to define management information for computer systems, networks, applications and services, and then use these management definitions to exchange information between different types of computers, including computers running non-Windows operating systems.

Currently, CIM modules can only be defined in a special type of XML file called a Cmdlet Definition XML (CDXML) file. Cmdlets and other features in CDXML files are defined using non-managed code assemblies. CIM modules can make use of CIM classes, the CIM .NET Framework, CIM management cmdlets, and WMI providers.

In Windows and Windows Server, support for CIM is implemented in the CimCmdlets module. If you enter **get-command –module cimcmdlets**, you'll find the module includes the following cmdlets:

- Export-BinaryMiLog
- Get-CimAssociatedInstance
- Get-CimClass
- Get-CimInstance
- Get-CimSession
- Import-BinaryMiLog
- Invoke-CimMethod
- New-CimInstance
- New-CimSession
- New-CimSessionOption
- Register-CimIndicationEvent

- Remove-CimInstance
- Remove-CimSession
- Set-CimInstance

CDXML files specify the mapping between Windows PowerShell cmdlets and CIM class operations and methods. CIM cmdlets call a CIM Object Manager (CIMOM) server, such as WMI in Windows, to manage a remote computer.

As long as a remote computer or device supports CIM and has a compliant CIMOM, you can work with the computer or device remotely using Windows PowerShell. This means that not only can you use CimCmdlets to manage Windows 8 or later and Windows Server 2012 or later, you also can use CimCmdlets to manage earlier releases of Windows and non-Windows computers.

You use New-CimSession to create a session with one or more remote computers, as shown in the following example:

```
$s = New-CimSession -ComputerName Server41, Server13,
Server39
```

However, if a computer or device does not have the Windows Management Framework, the CIM session can't be established using the standard approach, which relies on Windows Remote Management (WinRM). In this case, you must establish the session using the Distributed Component Object Model (DCOM) protocol. Additionally, as CIM sessions aren't implemented in PowerShell 2.0, you also must use DCOM if you want to work with computers with PowerShell 2.0 installed.

To use DCOM instead of WinRM, you must pass in a CimSessionOption object with the Protocol set when you create the session, as shown in this example:

```
$sopt = New-CimSessionOption -Protocol DCOM

$s = New-CimSession -ComputerName Server41, Server13,
Server39 -SessionOption $sopt
```

Here, the first command creates a CimSessionOption object and sets the protocol to DCOM and the second command creates a CIM Session with this option.

Once the remote CIM session is established, you use the CIM-related cmdlets to work with the remote systems and devices. Some cmdlets, such as Get-Module, also have CIM-related parameters that you can use.

In the following example, you use Get-CimInstance to examine the properties of the Win32_Processor object on the remote computers:

```
Get-CimInstance -ClassName Win32_Processor -CimSession $s
|fl
```

Here, you specify the CIM session you want to work with using the –CimSession parameter and list the properties of the Win32_Processor object on each computer so you can determine their processor type. You could just as easily examine the properties of the Win32_OperatingSystem, Win32_ComputerSystem or any other CIM object that is available in the session.

Because Windows Management Instrumentation (WMI), which is used to manage Windows resources and components, is a CIMOM server service that implements the CIM standard on Windows, you can use CIM cmdlets to work with MI objects as well. The CIM cmdlets show instances and classes from the default namespace (root/cimv2), unless you specify a different namespace to work with. For example, if you enter **get-cimclass** without specifying another namespace, you'll see a list of all classes in the root/cimv2 namespace.

> **TIP** Working with MI objects is covered extensively in Chapters 14 to 17. When managing remote computers, you may find that working with CIM cmdlets is easier than working with WMI cmdlets. The reason for this is that the CIM cmdlets make it easier to discover and work with Windows resources and components. An added advantage of working with CIM is efficiency. When you establish a persistent session, you work within the context of this session and the computers don't need to repeatedly establish, provision and remove connections.

When you are finished working with CIM, use Remove-CimSession to close the session to free the resources used. Here is an example:

```
Remove-CimSession $s
```

Chapter 11. Working Remotely Without WinRM

Some cmdlets have a –ComputerName parameter that lets you work with a remote computer without using Windows PowerShell remoting. This means you can use the cmdlet on any computer that is running Windows PowerShell, even if the computer is not configured for Windows PowerShell remoting. These cmdlets include the following:

- Get-WinEvent, Get-HotFix, Get-Counter
- Get-EventLog, Clear-EventLog, Write-EventLog, Limit-EventLog
- Show-EventLog, New-EventLog, Remove-EventLog
- Get-WmiObject, Get-Process, Get-Service, Set-Service
- Restart-Computer, Stop-Computer, Add-Computer
- Remove-Computer, Rename-Computer

Because these cmdlets don't use remoting, you can run any of these cmdlets on a remote computer in a domain simply by specifying the name of one or more remote computers in the –ComputerName parameter. However, Windows policies and configuration settings must allow remote connections, and you must still have the appropriate credentials.

The following command runs Get-WinEvent on PrintServer35 and FileServer17:

```
get-winevent –computername printserver35, fileserver17
```

When you use the –ComputerName parameter, these cmdlets return objects that include the name of the computer that generated the data. The remote computer name is stored in the MachineName property. Typically, the MachineName property is not displayed by default. The following example shows how you can use the Format-Table cmdlet to add the MachineName property to the output:

```
$procs = {get-process -computername Server56, Server42,
Server27 | sort-object -property Name}

&$procs | format-table Name, Handles, WS, CPU, MachineName -
auto
```

Name	Handles	WS	CPU	MachineName
acrotray	52	3948544	0	Server56
AlertService	139	7532544		Server56
csrss	594	20463616		Server56
csrss	655	5283840		Server56
CtHelper	96	6705152	0.078125	Server56
. . .				
acrotray	43	3948234	0	Server42
AlertService	136	7532244		Server42
csrss	528	20463755		Server42
csrss	644	5283567		Server42
CtHelper	95	6705576	0.067885	Server42
acrotray	55	3967544	0	Server27
AlertService	141	7566662		Server27
csrss	590	20434342		Server27
csrss	654	5242340		Server27
CtHelper	92	6705231	0.055522	Server27

You can get a complete list of all cmdlets with a –ComputerName parameter by typing the following command: **get-help * -parameter ComputerName**. To determine whether the –ComputerName parameter of a particular cmdlet requires Windows PowerShell remoting, display the parameter description by typing **get-help *CmdletName* -parameter ComputerName**, where *CmdletName* is the actual name of the cmdlet, such as

```
get-help Restart-Computer -parameter ComputerName
```

Typically, if the parameter doesn't require remoting, this is stated explicitly. For example, the output often states specifically:

```
This parameter does not rely on Windows PowerShell remoting.
You can use the -ComputerName parameter even if your
computer is not configured to run remote commands.
```

Chapter 12. Creating Background Jobs

PowerShell supports both local and remote background jobs. A background job is a command that you run asynchronously without interacting with it. When you start a background job, the command prompt returns immediately, and you can continue to work in the session while the job runs, even if it runs for an extended period of time.

Using Background Jobs

PowerShell runs background jobs on the local computer by default. You can run background jobs on remote computers by

- Starting an interactive session with a remote computer and starting a job in the interactive session. This approach allows you to work with the background job the same way as you would on the local computer.
- Running a background job on a remote computer that returns results to the local computer. This approach allows you to collect the results of background jobs and maintain them from your computer.
- Running a background job on a remote computer and maintaining the results on the remote computer. This approach helps ensure the job data is secure.

PowerShell has several commands for working with background jobs. These commands include

- **Get-Job**   Gets objects that represent the background jobs started in the current session. Without parameters, Get-Job returns a list of all jobs in the current session. The job object returned does not contain the job results. To get the results, use the Receive-Job cmdlet. You can use the parameters of Get-Job to get background jobs by their command text, names, IDs, or instance IDs. For command text, type the command or the part of the command with wildcards. For IDs, type an integer value that uniquely identifies the job in the current session. For names, type the friendly names previously assigned to the job. An instance ID is a GUID that uniquely identifies a job, even when you have multiple jobs running in PowerShell. To find the names, IDs, or instance IDs of jobs, use Get-Jobs without parameters. You can use the –State parameter to get only jobs in the specified state. Valid values are NotStarted, Running, Completed, Stopped, Failed, and Blocked. Use the –Before or –After parameters to get jobs completed before or after a specified date and time.

▪ **Receive-Job** Gets the output and errors of the PowerShell background jobs started in the current session. You can get the results of all jobs or identify jobs by their name, ID, instance ID, computer name, location, or session, or by inputting a job object. By default, job results are deleted after you receive them, but you can use the –Keep parameter to save the results so that you can receive them again. To delete the job results, receive them again without the –Keep parameter, close the session, or use the Remove-Job cmdlet to delete the job from the session.

▪ **Remove-Job** Deletes PowerShell background jobs that were started by using Start-Job or the –AsJob parameter of a cmdlet. Without parameters or parameter values, Remove-Job has no effect. You can delete all jobs or selected jobs based on their command, name, ID, instance ID, or state, or by passing a job object to Remove-Job. Before deleting a running job, you should use Stop-Job to stop the job. If you try to delete a running job, Remove-Job fails. You can use the –Force parameter to delete a running job. If you do not delete a background job, the job remains in the global job cache until you close the session

- **Start-Job** Starts a Windows PowerShell background job on the local computer. To run a background job on a remote computer, use the –AsJob parameter of a cmdlet that supports background jobs, or use the Invoke-Command cmdlet to run a Start-Job command on the remote computer. When you start a Windows PowerShell background job, the job starts, but the results do not appear immediately. Instead, the command returns an object that represents the background job. The job object contains useful information about the job, but it does not contain the results. This approach allows you to continue working while the job runs.
- **Stop-Job** Stops PowerShell background jobs that are in progress. You can stop all jobs or stop selected jobs based on their name, ID, instance ID, or state, or by passing a job object to Stop-Job. When you stop a background job, PowerShell completes all tasks that are pending in that job queue and then ends the job. No new tasks are added to the queue after you stop the job. Stop-Job does not delete background jobs. To delete a job, use Remove-Job.
- **Wait-Job** Waits for PowerShell background jobs to complete before it displays the command prompt. You can wait until any specific background jobs are complete or until all background jobs are complete. Use the –Timeout parameter to set a maximum wait time for the job. When the commands in the job are complete, Wait-Job displays the command prompt and returns a job object so that you can pipe it to another command. Use the –Any parameter to display the command prompt when any job completes. By default, Wait-Job waits until all of the specified jobs are complete before displaying the prompt.

Some cmdlets can be run as background jobs automatically using an –AsJob parameter. You can get a complete list of all cmdlets with an –AsJob parameter by typing the following command: **get-help * - parameter AsJob**. These cmdlets include:

- **Invoke-Command**   Runs commands on local and remote computers.
- **Invoke-WmiMethod**   Calls Windows Management Instrumentation (WMI) methods.
- **Test-Connection**   Sends Internet Control Message Protocol (ICMP) echo request packets (*pings*) to one or more computers.
- **Restart-Computer**   Restarts (*reboots*) the operating system on local and remote computers.
- **Stop-Computer**   Stops (shuts down) local and remote computers.

The basic way background jobs work is as follows:

1. You start a background job using Start-Job or the –AsJob parameter of a cmdlet.
2. The job starts, but the results do not appear immediately. Instead, the command returns an object that represents the background job.
3. As necessary, you work with the job object. The job object contains useful information about the job, but it does not contain the results. This approach allows you to continue working while the job runs.
4. To view the results of a job started in the current session, you use Receive-Job. You can identify jobs by their name, ID, instance ID, computer name, location, or session, or by inputting a job object to Receive-Job. After you receive a job, the job results are deleted (unless you use the –Keep parameter).

Starting Jobs in Interactive Sessions

You can start a background job in any interactive session. The procedure for starting a background job is almost the same whether you are working with your local computer or a remote computer. When you work with the local computer, all operations occur on the local computer. When you work with a remote computer, all operations occur on the remote computer.

You can use the Enter-PSSession cmdlet to start an interactive session with a remote computer. Use the –ComputerName parameter to specify the name of the remote computer, such as in the following:

```
enter-pssession -computername filesvr32
```

> **NOTE**   To end the interactive session later, type **exit-pssession**.

You start a background job in a local or remote session using the Start-Job cmdlet. You can reference a script block with the –ScriptBlock parameter or a local script using the –FilePath parameter.

The following command runs a background job that gets the events in the System, Application, and Security logs. Because Start-Job returns an object that represents the job, this command saves the job object in the $job variable. Type the command as a single line:

```
$job = start-job -scriptblock {$share =
"\\FileServer85\logs";
$logs = "system","application","security";
foreach ($log in $logs) { $filename =
"$env:computername".ToUpper() + "$log" + "log" +
(get-date -format yyyyMMdd) + ".log";
Get-EventLog $log | set-content $share\$filename; }
}
```

Or use the back apostrophe to continue the line as shown here:

```
$job = start-job -scriptblock {$share =
"\\FileServer85\logs"; `
$logs = "system","application","security"; `
foreach ($log in $logs) { `
$filename = "$env:computername".ToUpper() + "$log" + "log" +
`
(get-date -format yyyyMMdd) + ".log"; `
Get-EventLog $log | set-content $share\$filename; } `
}
```

Alternatively, you can store the commands as a script on the local computer and then reference the local script using the –FilePath parameter as shown in the examples that follow.

Command line
```
$job = start-job -filepath c:\scripts\eventlogs.ps1
```

Source for Eventlogs.ps1
```
$share = "\\FileServer85\logs"
$logs = "system","application","security"

foreach ($log in $logs) {
   $filename = "$env:computername".ToUpper() + "$log" + "log"
+ `
(get-date -format yyyyMMdd) + ".log"
   Get-EventLog $log | set-content $share\$filename
}
```

The script must reside on the local computer or in a directory that the local computer can access. When you use FilePath, Windows PowerShell converts the contents of the specified script file to a script block and runs the script block as a background job.

While the job runs, you can continue working and run other commands, including other background jobs. However, you must keep the interactive session open until the job completes. Otherwise, the jobs will be interrupted, and the results will be lost.

> **NOTE** You don't have to store Job objects in variables. However, doing so makes it easier to work with Job objects. But if you do use variables and you run multiple jobs, be sure that you store the returned Job objects in different variables, such as $job1, $job2, and $job3.

You use the Get-Job cmdlet to do the following:

- Find out if a job is complete.
- Display the command passed to the job.
- Get information about jobs so that you can work with them.

You can get all jobs or identify jobs by their name, ID, instance ID, computer name, location, or session, or by inputting a job object. PowerShell gives jobs sequential IDs and names automatically. The first job you run has an ID of 1 and a name of Job1, the second job you run has an ID of 2 and a name of Job2, and so on. You can also name jobs when you start them using the –Name parameter. In the following example, you create a job named Logs:

```
start-job -filepath c:\scripts\eventlogs.ps1 -name Logs
```

You can then get information about this job using Get-Job and –Name as shown in the following example and sample output:

```
get-job -name Logs
Id   Name   State   HasMoreData   Location   Command
--   ----   -----   -----------   --------   -------
```

```
1   Logs  Failed  False              filesvr32  $share =
"\\FileServer...
```

Because this job failed to run, you won't necessarily be able to receive its output or error results. You can, however, take a closer look at the job information. For more detailed information, you need to format the output in a list as shown in this example and sample output:

```
get-job -name logs | format-list
```

```
HasMoreData    : False
StatusMessage  :
Location       : filesvr32
Command        : $share = "\\FileServer85\logs"; $logs =
"system", "application","security"; foreach ($log in $logs)
{
$filename = "$env:computername".ToUpper() + "$log" + "log" +
(get-date -format yyyyMMdd) + ".log"; Get-EventLog $log |
set-content $share\$filename; }
JobStateInfo   : Failed
Finished       : System.Threading.ManualResetEvent
InstanceId     : 679ed475-4edd-4ba5-ae79-e1e9b3aa590e
Id             : 3
Name           : Logs
ChildJobs      : {Job4}
Output         : {}
Error          : {}
Progress       : {}
Verbose        : {}
Debug          : {}
Warning        : {}
```

If you are running several jobs, type **get-job** to check the status of all jobs as shown in the following example and sample output:

```
get-job
Id Name    State     HasMoreData  Location  Command
-- ----    -----     -----------  --------  -------
```

```
1  Job1   Completed  False        localhost   $share =
"\\FileServer...
3  Job3   Running    True         localhost   $logs =
"system","appl...
```

When a job completes, you can use the Receive-Job cmdlet to get the results of the job. However, keep in mind that if a job doesn't produce output or errors to the PowerShell prompt, there won't be any results to receive.

You can receive the results of all jobs by typing **receive-job**, or you can identify jobs by their name, ID, instance ID, computer name, location, or session, or by inputting a job object. The following example receives results by name:

```
receive-job -name Job1, Job3
```

The following example receives results by ID:

```
receive-job -id 1, 3
```

Job results are deleted automatically after you receive them. Use the –Keep parameter to save the results so that you can receive them again. To delete the job results, receive the job results again without the –Keep parameter, close the session, or use the Remove-Job cmdlet to delete the job from the session.

Alternatively, you can write the job results to a file. The following example writes the job results to C:\logs\mylog.txt:

```
receive-job -name Job1 > c:\logs\mylog.txt
```

When working with a remote computer, keep in mind that this command runs on the remote computer. As a result, the file is created on the remote computer. If you are using one log for multiple jobs, be sure to use the append operator as shown in this example:

```
receive-job -name Job1 >> c:\logs\mylog.txt
receive-job -name Job2 >> c:\logs\mylog.txt
receive-job -name Job3 >> c:\logs\mylog.txt
```

While in the current session with the remote computer, you can view the contents of the results file by typing the following command:

```
get-content c:\logs\mylog.txt
```

If you close the session with the remote computer, you can use Invoke-Command to view the file on the remote computer as shown here:

```
$ms = new-pssession -computername fileserver84

invoke-command -session $ms -scriptblock {get-content
c:\logs\mylog.txt}
```

Running Jobs Noninteractively

Rather than working in an interactive session, you can use the Invoke-Command cmdlet with the –AsJob parameter to start background jobs and return results to the local computer. When you use the –AsJob parameter, the job object is created on the local computer, even though the job runs on the remote computer. When the job completes, the results are returned to the local computer.

In the following example, we create a noninteractive PowerShell session with three remote computers and then use Invoke-Command to run a background job that gets the events in the System, Application, and Security logs. This is the same job created earlier, only now the job runs on all the computers listed in the –ComputerName parameter. Type the command as a single line:

```
$s = new-pssession -computername fileserver34, dataserver18
Invoke-command –session $s -asjob -scriptblock {$share =
"\\FileServer85\logs";
$logs = "system","application","security";
foreach ($log in $logs) {
$filename = "$env:computername".ToUpper() + "$log" + "log" +
(get-date -format yyyyMMdd) + ".log";
Get-EventLog $log | set-content $share\$filename; }
}
```

Or use the back apostrophe to continue the line as shown here:

```
$s = new-pssession -computername fileserver34, dataserver18
`
Invoke-command –session $s `
-asjob -scriptblock {$share = "\\FileServer85\logs"; `
$logs = "system","application","security"; `
foreach ($log in $logs) { `
$filename = "$env:computername".ToUpper() + "$log" + `
"log" + (get-date -format yyyyMMdd) + ".log"; `
Get-EventLog $log | set-content $share\$filename; } `
}
```

Alternatively, you can store the commands as a script on the local computer and then reference the local script using the –FilePath parameter as shown in the examples that follow.

Command line

```
$s = new-pssession -computername fileserver34, dataserver18
Invoke-command –session $s -asjob -filepath
c:\scripts\eventlogs.ps1
```

Source for Eventlogs.ps1

```
$share = "\\FileServer85\logs"
$logs = "system","application","security"

foreach ($log in $logs) {
   $filename = "$env:computername".ToUpper() + "$log" + "log"
+   `
(get-date -format yyyyMMdd) + ".log"
   Get-EventLog $log | set-content $share\$filename
}
```

The script must reside on the local computer or in a directory that the local computer can access. As before, when you use FilePath, Windows PowerShell converts the contents of the specified script file to a script block and runs the script block as a background job.

Now, you don't necessarily have to run Invoke-Command via a noninteractive session. However, the advantage of doing so is that you can now work with the job objects running in the session. For example, to get information about the jobs on all three computers, you type the following command:

```
get-job
```

To receive job results you type this command:

```
receive-job -keep
```

Or you can type the following if you want to save the results to a file on the local computer:

```
receive-job > c:\logs\mylog.txt
```

A variation on this technique is to use the Invoke-Command cmdlet to run the Start-Job cmdlet. This technique allows you to run background jobs on multiple computers and keep the results on the remote computers. Here's how this works:

1. You use Invoke-Command without the –AsJob parameter to run the Start-Job cmdlet.
2. A job object is created on each remote computer.
3. Commands in the job are run separately on each remote computer.
4. Job results are maintained separately on each remote computer.
5. You work with the job objects and results on each remote computer separately.

Here, you use Invoke-Command to start jobs on three computers and store the Job objects in the $j variable:

```
$s = new-pssession -computername fileserver34, dataserver18
```

```
$j = invoke-command –session $s {start-job –filepath
c:\scripts\elogs.ps1}
```

Again, you don't necessarily have to run Invoke-Command via a noninteractive session. However, the advantage of doing so is that you can now work with the job objects running on all three computers via the session. For example, to get information about the jobs on all three computers, you type the following command:

```
invoke-command -session $s -scriptblock {get-job}
```

Or, because you stored the Job objects in the $j variable, you also could enter:

```
$j
```

To receive job results, you type this command:

```
invoke-command -session $s -scriptblock { param($j) receive-
job -job $j -keep} -argumentlist $j
```

Or you can do the following if you want to save the results to a file on each remote computer:

```
invoke-command -session $s -command {param($j) receive-job -
job $j > c:\logs\mylog.txt} -argumentlist $j
```

In both examples, you use Invoke-Command to run a Receive-Job command in each session in $s. Because $j is a local variable, the script block uses the "param" keyword to declare the variable in the command and the ArgumentList parameter to supply the value of $j.

Chapter 13. Creating Scheduled Jobs

With Windows PowerShell, you also can create scheduled jobs, which combine the best features of both PowerShell background jobs and Task Scheduler tasks. As scheduled job cmdlets are included in the PSScheduledJob module, you can enter **get-command –module psscheduledjob** to list all the related cmdlets. You use these commands to create, edit, and modify scheduled jobs, job triggers, and job options.

As scheduled jobs are an enhancement for Windows PowerShell 3.0 and later, the basic commands for working with background jobs have also been extended to work with scheduled jobs. This means you can use Start-Job, Stop-Job, Get-Job, Receive-Job, Remove-Job, and Wait-Job to work with scheduled jobs as well.

Scheduled jobs rely on the Task Scheduler service to monitor the system state and clock. This service must be running and properly configured for job scheduling to work. Like background jobs, scheduled jobs run asynchronously in the background. Creating a schedule jobs requires:

1. Defining one or more job triggers. You create job triggers using New-JobTrigger. You manage Job Trigger objects using Get-JobTrigger, Add-JobTrigger, Enable-JobTrigger, Disable-JobTrigger, Set-JobTrigger, and Remove-JobTrigger.

2. Setting job options as appropriate. You create job options using New-ScheduledJobOption. You manage Job Option objects using Get-ScheduledJobOption and Set-ScheduledJobOption.

3. Registering and running the scheduled job. You register and run scheduled jobs using Register-ScheduledJob. You manage Scheduled Job objects using Get-ScheduledJob, Set-ScheduledJob,

Enable-ScheduledJob, Disable-ScheduledJob, and Unregister-ScheduledJob.

Processes related to each of these steps are discussed in the sections that follow. Before getting started, however, keep in mind that triggers and options can be specified directly when you register scheduled jobs or you can create related objects that can be passed to a job when you are registering it.

Defining Job Triggers

You create job triggers using the New-JobTrigger cmdlet. As the cmdlet returns an object, you usually store the object in a variable that is then passed to the scheduled job when you register it. Job triggers specify the circumstances under which a job begins and ends. You can begin a job based on a schedule as well as on computer startup and user logon. As job triggers based on startup and log on are the easiest to define, we'll look at those first.

Running Jobs at Startup or Logon

To create a job trigger based on computer startup, you use the –AtStartup parameter. The basic syntax is:

```
New-JobTrigger -AtStartup [-RandomDelay HH:MM:SS]
```

Where –RandomDelay sets the maximum interval for a random delay. In the following example, you create a trigger that runs at startup with a random delay of up to 30 minutes:

```
$tr = New-JobTrigger -AtStartup –RandomDelay 00:30:00
```

> **NOTE** Setting a random delay for jobs is a best practice whenever many users or computers may run a resource-intensive job at the same time. As all job triggers can use a random delay, I won't include the –RandomDelay parameter in the other syntax examples.
>
> **MORE INFO** Time-related values are set using TimeSpan objects or strings that PowerShell can convert automatically to TimeSpan objects. In syntax examples, I typically used the abbreviated syntax HH:MM:SS, which sets the hours, minutes and seconds in a time span. The full syntax, DD.HH:MM:SS, allows you to set day values as well. For example, 1.00:00:00 specifies a time span of 1 day and 2.00:00:00 sets a time span of 2 days.

To create a job trigger based on user logon, you use the –AtLogon parameter. The basic syntax is:

```
New-JobTrigger -AtLogon [-User [Domain\]UserName]
```

Where –User is an optional parameter that specifies the users who trigger the scheduled job. For workgroups and homegroups, users can be identified by their logon name, such as WilliamS. For domains, users should be identified by their logon name in Domain\UserName format, such as ImaginedL\WilliamS. To specify more than one user, enter the user names in a comma-separated list. To apply the trigger to all users, enter * or simply omit the –User parameter. In the following example, you create a trigger that applies only to WilliamS and store the Job Trigger object in the $tr variable:

```
$tr = New-JobTrigger -AtLogon -User ImaginedL\WilliamS
```

To confirm the settings of this job trigger, enter the following command:

```
$tr | fl
```

The resulting output shows the properties of the Job Trigger object stored in the $tr variable. You can make changes to the job trigger using Set-JobTrigger.

Running Jobs Daily or Weekly

In addition to jobs that run at startup or logon, you can create jobs that run daily or weekly. The basic syntax for a job trigger based on a daily run schedule is:

```
New-JobTrigger -Daily [-DaysInterval Int] -At DateTime
```

Where –DaysInterval specifies the number of days between schedules runs and –At specifies date and time to start the job. Keep the following in mind:

- With –DaysInterval, the default value is 1, meaning the scheduled job should run every day. If you specify any other value, the value determines the number of days between schedules runs. For example, a value of 2 specifies that the job should run every other day, a value of 3 specifies the job should run every third day, etc.
- With –At, you can use a DateTime object or any string that can be converted to a DateTime object. Although a string like "2/15/2015 4:50 AM" or "Feb 15, 2015 4:50" sets an exact date and time, you can use a partial value, such as "3:30 PM" or "4/18". When you only specify the time, the command creates a trigger using the current date. When you only specify a date, the command creates a trigger that runs at 12:00:00 AM on the specified date.

In the following example, you create a trigger that runs every other day, starting March 2, 2015 at 3:00:00 AM:

```
$eodt = New-JobTrigger -Daily -DaysInterval 2 -At "March 2,
2015 3:00:00 AM"
```

When you are creating jobs with a weekly run schedule, you specify the
number of weeks between run schedules using –WeeksInterval and the
days of the week to run using –DaysOfWeek, giving a basic syntax of:

```
New-JobTrigger -Weekly [-WeeksInterval Int] -At DateTime
-DaysOfWeek Day1, Day2, …
```

With –WeeksInterval, the default value is 1, meaning the scheduled job
should run every week. If you specify any other value, the value
determines the number of weeks between runs. For example, an interval
of 2 specifies that the job should run every other week, an interval of 3
specifies the job should run every third week, etc.

With –DaysOfWeek, you enter day names, such as Monday, or the integer
values 0 to 6, with 0 representing Sunday. With multiple run days, each
day name or value must be separated with a comma, as shown in the
following example where the job runs every week on Monday and
Thursday:

```
$etwt = New-JobTrigger -Weekly -WeeksInterval 1 -DaysOfWeek
Monday, Thursday -At "June 5, 2015 5:00:00 AM"
```

It's important to point out that if you enclose the day names in quotes,
each day name must be specified separately, such as:

```
"Tuesday", "Friday"
```

Creating Jobs that Run Once or Repeatedly

In addition to being able to create scheduled jobs that run daily or weekly, you can create scheduled jobs that run once and also optionally repeat at specific time intervals, such as every hour. The basic syntax is:

```
New-JobTrigger -Once [-RepeatIndefinitely] [-
RepetitionDuration DD.HH:MM:SS] [-RepetitionInterval
HH:MM:SS] -At DateTime
```

By default, Run Once jobs do not repeat. If you want a job to repeat, you must use –RepeatIndefinitely to allow a job trigger to repeat without having to set a repetition duration or you must specify an allowed duration for repeating the job. For example, to allow a job to run and repeat for 24 hours, you would set the –RepetitionDuration parameter to 24:00:00. For repeating jobs, you must also specify the repetition interval. For example, if you want a job to repeat every hour, you'd set the –RepetitionInterval to 01:00:00.

In the following example, you create a trigger that runs indefinitely at 3-hour intervals, starting June 1, 2015 at 6:30:00 AM:

```
$rt = New-JobTrigger -Once -RepeatIndefinitely
-RepetitionInterval 00:03:00 -At "June 1, 2015 6:30:00 AM"
```

Rather than running a job indefinitely, you may want a job to run for a specified period of time, such as 24 hours or 7 days. In the following example, you create a job that runs every 2 hours for 5 days:

```
$rt = New-JobTrigger -Once -RepetitionDuration 5.00:00:00
-RepetitionInterval 00:03:00 -At "June 1, 2015 6:30:00 AM"
```

Setting Job Options

You create job options using the New-ScheduledJobOption cmdlet. As the cmdlet returns an object, you usually store the object in a variable that is then passed to the scheduled job when you register it.

Understanding Job Option Parameters

Job options help qualify the conditions under which a job is started or stopped once it is triggered. You can use options to wake the computer to run a job, to specify whether the job runs when a network connection isn't available, and to specify whether a job runs only when AC power is available.

You also can use options to start, stop and restart a job based on the processor idle time. For example, you might want a job to start only if the processor has been idle for at least 5 minutes, stop if the processor is no longer idle, and then restart once the processor is again idle.

You specify job options using the following parameters:

- **–ContinueIfGoingOnBattery** Specifies that a running job should keep running if the computer switches to battery power.
- **–DoNotAllowDemandStart** Specifies that a job cannot be manually started by a user. Thus, the job can only run according to its defined schedule.
- **–HideInTaskScheduler** Creates the job as a hidden task in the Task Scheduler. As users can display hidden tasks in the Task Scheduler, this doesn't prevent users from seeing the scheduled job.
- **–IdleDuration *HH:MM:SS*** Specifies how long a computer must be idle before the job starts. The default is 10 minutes (00:10:00).

- **–IdleTimeout *HH:MM:SS***   Specifies how long a job waits for the computer to be idle. The default value is 1 hour (01:00:00). If the timeout elapses before the computer is idle, the job does not run at that scheduled run time. At the next scheduled run time, the Task Scheduler will again evaluate the computer's idle status and determine whether the job should run.
- **–MultipleInstancePolicy *PolicyType***   Determines how the Task Scheduler handles a request to start a new instance of a scheduled job while another instance of the job is already running. Policy type values you can use are: IgnoreNew, Parallel, Queue, and StopExisting. As the value IgnoreNew is the default, the currently running instance of the job continues execution and a request to start a new instance of that job is ignored.
- **–RequireNetwork**   Runs the job only when the computer has a valid and available network connection. If a network is not available, the job does not run at that scheduled run time. At the next scheduled run time, the Task Scheduler will again evaluate the status of network connections and determine whether the job should run.
- **–RestartOnIdleResume**   If you use –StopIfGoingOffIdle, you can use this parameter to specify that the computer should restart a scheduled job when the computer is again idle.
- **–RunElevated**   Runs the job with elevated, administrator permissions. If you use this option, you should also schedule the job using specific credentials and those credentials must have appropriate administrator permissions.
- **–StartIfIdle**   Starts the job if the computer has been idle for the time specified in the IdleDuration, as long as the IdleTimeout has not elapsed.
- **–StartIfOnBattery**   Starts the job if the computer is on battery power.

- **–StopIfGoingOffIdle**   Stops the job if the computer becomes active while the job is running. A computer becomes active when it is being used by a user. By default, a job that is suspended when a computer becomes active resumes when the computer is idle again. If you don't want this to happen, set –RestartOnIdleResume to $False.
- **–WakeToRun**   Wakes the computer from a Hibernate or Sleep state at the scheduled start time so the job can run. If you don't use this parameter, the Task Scheduler will not wake the computer.

Using these options, the basic syntax for New-ScheduledJobOption is:

```
New-ScheduledJobOption [-ContinueIfGoingOnBattery]
[-DoNotAllowDemandStart] [-HideInTaskScheduler]
[-IdleDuration HH:MM:SS] [-IdleTimeout HH:MM:SS]
[-MultipleInstancePolicy PolicyType] [-RequireNetwork]
[-RestartOnIdleResume] [-RunElevated] [-StartIfIdle]
[-StartIfOnBattery] [-StopIfGoingOffIdle] [-WakeToRun]
```

Working with Job Options

By default, jobs created using Register-ScheduledJob:

- Can be started manually by users.
- Are displayed in the Task Scheduler.
- Run with the standard permissions of the user who created the job.
- Start only if a computer is on AC power and stop if the computer switches to battery power.
- Run whether a computer has a network connection or is idle.
- Do not run if a computer is in the Sleep or Hibernate state.
- Only allow one instance of a job to run at a time.

If you want a job to run with different options, you must specify these options when you create the job or pass in a Scheduled Job Option object with the desired options.

- Use –DoNotAllowDemandStart to prevent users from manually starting a job.
- Use –HideInTaskScheduler to create a hidden job rather than a standard job.
- Use –RunElevated to run the job with elevated, administrator permissions rather than the standard permissions of the user who created the job.
- Use –StartIfOnBattery to allow a job to start when the computer is on battery power and –ContinueIfGoingOnBattery to allow a job to continue running if a computer switches from AC power to battery power while the job is running.
- Use –WakeToRun to allow the Task Scheduler to wake the computer to run the job.

Not all of the options are simple switch parameters, however. To control multiple instances of jobs, you must use –MultipleInstancePolicy to specify the policy type to use. Although the default policy, IgnoreNew, simply ignores any request to start another instance of a currently running job, the other policy types give you more control. The other options are:

- **Parallel**   With Parallel, Task Scheduler allows multiple instances of jobs to run at the same time.
- **Queue**   With Queue, Task Scheduler queues additional requests to run a job and then runs each in turn when the current instance finishes running.
- **StopExisting**   With StopExisting, Task Scheduler stops the currently running instance and starts the new instance of the job.

In the following example, you define job options that allow multiple instances of a job to run at the same time and also ensure the job runs regardless of the power state:

```
$opts = New-ScheduledJobOption -MultipleInstancePolicy
Parallel
-StartIfOnBattery -ContinueIfGoingOnBattery
```

To confirm these job options, enter the following command:

```
$opts | fl
```

The resulting output shows the properties of the Scheduled Job Option object stored in the $opts variable. You can make changes to the job options using Set-ScheduledJobOption.

If you want a job to run regardless of whether a computer is idle or active, you need only accept the default job options. To start a job only if a computer is idle, you use –StartIfIdle and optionally specify an idle duration and idle timeout. To stop a job if a computer ceases to be idle, add –StopIfGoingOffIdle. To restart a stopped job when a computer resumes an idle state, you must add –RestartOnIdleResume. Rather than using these parameters separately, these parameters are most often used together to ensure scheduled jobs work as expected with idling, as shown in the following example:

```
$joptions = New-ScheduledJobOption -StartIfIdle
-StopIfGoingOffIdle -RestartOnIdleResume
```

Here, you define job options that start a job only if the computer has been idle for 10 minutes and the Task Scheduler hasn't waited more than 1 hour for the computer to enter the idle state. If the computer ceases to be idle, Task Scheduler stops the job, and waits for the computer to resume the idle state before restarting the job. Use the –IdleDuration and – IdleTimeout parameters to override the default idle duration and timeout.

Registering and Running Scheduled Jobs

After you define job triggers and options, you use Register-ScheduledJob to create the job and register it with Task Scheduler. Current jobs configured on a computer are accessible through the Task Scheduler application, which provides a graphical interface for the Task Scheduler service and jobs that have been registered in the Task Scheduler Library.

On Windows desktops, you can access the Task Scheduler application in Computer Management. On Windows servers, select Task Scheduler on the Tools menu in Server Manager to open the Task Scheduler application. As shown in the figure that follows, jobs registered using PowerShell are displayed in the Task Scheduler Library under Microsoft\Windows\PowerShell\ScheduledJobs.

You have two options for specifying the commands a scheduled job executes. You can specify the commands to run using a script block and the following basic syntax:

Register-ScheduledJob [-Name] *JobName* [-ScriptBlock] { *ScriptBlock* } [-Credential *Credential*] [-RunNow] [-ScheduledJobOption *Options*] [-Trigger *Triggers*]

Or you can specify the full path to a script to run using the following basic syntax:

Register-ScheduledJob [-Name] *JobName* [-FilePath] *FilePath*
[-Credential *Credential*] [-RunNow] [-ScheduledJobOption *Options*]
[-Trigger *Triggers*]

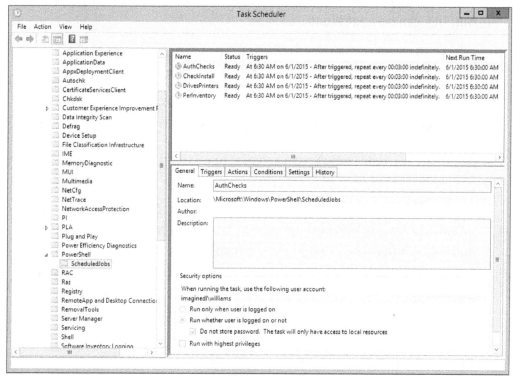

Scheduled jobs are registered in Task Scheduler.

With script blocks, the curly braces { } denote the start and end of the block of commands to run and you use semicolon to specify where one command ends and another begins, such as:

```
$tr = New-JobTrigger -Weekly -WeeksInterval 4 -DaysOfWeek
Tuesday, Thursday -At "June 5, 2015 5:00:00 AM"

$opts = New-ScheduledJobOption -StartIfOnBattery
-ContinueIfGoingOnBattery -RunElevated
```

```
Register-ScheduledJob -Name SysChecks -ScriptBlock {
get-process > ./processes.txt; get-eventlog system >
./events.txt} -ScheduledJobOption $opts -Trigger $tr
```

With scripts, you must specify the complete path to the script you want to run. This can be a local path, such as:

```
Register-ScheduledJob -Name SysChecks -FilePath
D:\Scripts\SysChecks.ps1 -ScheduledJobOption
$opts -Trigger $tr
```

Or a UNC path available to the user under which the process runs, such as:

```
Register-ScheduledJob -Name SysChecks -FilePath
\\Server48\Scripts\SysChecks.ps1 -ScheduledJobOption
$opts -Trigger $tr
```

When you are working with remote computers, you can create a session and register the scheduled job using Invoke-Command. As shown in the following example, the techniques used are similar to those discussed previously:

```
$cred = Get-Credential

$ses = New-PSSession -ComputerName (Get-Content
.\Computers.txt) -Credential $cred

invoke-command -session $s { $tr = New-JobTrigger -Daily
-DaysInterval 2 -At "March 31, 2015 5:00:00 AM";
$opt = New-ScheduledJobOption -StopIfGoingOffIdle
-StartIfIdle -RestartOnIdleResume; Register-ScheduledJob
-Name SysChecks -FilePath "\\Server33\Scripts\CheckSys.ps1"
-ScheduledJobOption $opts -Trigger $tr}
```

Here, you establish a PowerShell session with the computers listed in the Computers.txt file, and then you invoke commands on each of those remote computers so that you can create a scheduled job called

SysChecks on those computers. Because the jobs are created on remote computers, you must access the remote computers to check the status of the jobs and view any related results. It's important to note that you should define the job triggers and job options using commands invoked on the remote computers. If you don't do this, the objects aren't available for your use on those computers.

An alternative to working with invoked commands would be to create a PowerShell session and then import the session. You could then work directly with the remote computers, as shown in the following example:

```
$cred = Get-Credential

$ses = New-PSSession -ComputerName (Get-Content
.\Computers.txt) -Credential $cred

Import-PSSession -Session $ses -AllowClobber

$tr = New-JobTrigger -Daily -DaysInterval 2 -At "March 31,
2015 5:00:00 AM"

$opt = New-ScheduledJobOption -StopIfGoingOffIdle -
StartIfIdle -RestartOnIdleResume

Register-ScheduledJob -Name SysChecks -FilePath
"\\Server33\Scripts\CheckSys.ps1" -ScheduledJobOption
$opts -Trigger $tr
```

Modifying and Removing Scheduled Jobs

After you create a scheduled job, you'll often need to manage it, which means:

- Using Get-ScheduledJob to view scheduled jobs.

- Using Disable-ScheduledJob to disable a job when it is temporarily not needed.
- Using Enable-ScheduledJob to enable a job that was previously disabled.
- Using Set-ScheduledJob to modify job settings.
- Using Unregister-ScheduledJob to remove scheduled jobs that are no longer needed.

> **NOTE**   You can only work with scheduled jobs created by the current user. You can't work with jobs created by other users or any other scheduled tasks available in Task Scheduler.
>
> **MORE INFO**   The only way to work with jobs created in PowerShell by other users is to use the credentials of that user. That said, if you need to remove jobs created by other users and don't have the credentials to do this, you can remove the jobs in the Task Scheduler application, provided you have administrator permissions. In Task Scheduler, navigate the Task Scheduler Library to Microsoft\Windows\PowerShell\ScheduledJobs. Select a job that you want to delete and then press the Delete key. When prompted to confirm the action, select Yes.
>
> Tasks Scheduler also allows you to delete tasks using the Actions pane. In the Actions pane, make sure you don't select Delete Folder (which is listed under ScheduledJobs and likely the first delete option). Instead, choose the Delete option under Selected Item.

Get-ScheduledJob returns information about jobs scheduled on a computer. If you enter the command without options, information about all the jobs you scheduled via PowerShell are listed. If you add the –Name or –Id parameter, you can get information about a specific job by name or ID number.

As Get-ScheduledJob doesn't have a –ComputerName parameter, you can only view information about jobs on computers to which you are connected. Thus, if you are working in a remote session, Get-ScheduledJob returns information about the computers you've connected to in the remote session. Otherwise, Get-ScheduledJob returns information only about jobs on the local computer.

Enable-ScheduledJob, Disable-ScheduledJob and Unregister-ScheduledJob work in much the same way as Get-ScheduledJob. Add the –Name or –Id parameter to specify the job you want to work with by name or ID number. In this example, you enable the HTasks scheduled job which was previously registered and disabled by the current user:

```
Enable-ScheduledJob HTasks
```

If you don't specify a job by name or ID number, you may accidentally modify all jobs created by the current user. Consider the following example:

```
Get-ScheduledJob | Enable-ScheduledJob
```

Here, you enable all scheduled jobs previously registered and disabled by the current user. Keep in mind that if you are working in a remote session, these commands modify jobs defined on the computers you've connected to in the remote session. Otherwise, these commands modify jobs on the local computer.

Chapter 14. Object Essentials

In Windows PowerShell, objects do the real work. As data moves from one command to the next, it moves as it does within objects. Essentially, this means that objects are simply collections of data that represent items in defined namespaces.

Understanding Objects

All objects have a type, state, and behavior. The type provides details about what the object represents. For example, an object that represents a system process is a Process object. The state of an object pertains to data elements and their associated values. Everything the object knows about these elements and values describes the state of the object. Data elements associated with objects are stored in properties.

The behavior of an object depends on the actions the object can perform on the item that the object represents. In object-oriented terminology, this construct is called a *method*. A method belongs to the object class it is a member of, and you use a method when you need to perform a specific action on an object. For example, the Process object includes a method for stopping the process. You can use this method to halt execution of the process that the object represents.

Putting this together, you can see that the state of an object depends on the things the object knows, and the behavior of the object depends on the actions the object can perform. Objects encapsulate properties and related methods into a single identifiable unit. Therefore, objects are easy to reuse, update, and maintain.

Object classes encapsulate objects. A single class can be used to instantiate multiple objects. This means that you can have many active objects or instances of a class. By encapsulating objects within a class structure, you can group sets of objects by type. For example, when you type **get-process** at the PowerShell prompt, PowerShell returns a collection of objects representing all processing that are running on the computer. Although all the objects are returned together in a single collection, each object is separate, retaining its own states and behaviors.

PowerShell supports several dozen object types. When you combine commands in a pipeline, the commands pass information to each other as objects. When the first command runs, it sends one or more objects of a particular class along the pipeline to the second command. The second command receives the collection of objects from the first command, processes the objects, and then either displays output or passes new or modified objects to the next command in the pipeline. This continues until all commands in the pipeline run and the final command's output is displayed.

You can examine the properties and methods of any object by sending the output through the Get-Member cmdlet. For example, system processes and services are represented by the Process and Service objects, respectively. To determine the properties and methods of a Process object, you type **get-process | get-member**. To determine the properties and methods of a Service object, you type **get-service | get-member**. In both instances, the pipe character (|) sends the output of the first cmdlet to the Get-Member cmdlet, and Get-Member shows you the formal type of the object class and a complete listing of its members, as shown in the following example and sample output:

```
get-service | get-member
```

```
     TypeName: System.ServiceProcess.ServiceController

Name                      MemberType      Definition
----                      ----------      ----------
Name                      AliasProperty   Name = ServiceName
Disposed                  Event           System.EventHandler
Disposed
Close                     Method          System.Void Close()
  .  .  .
CanPauseAndContinue   Property   System.Boolean CanPauseAndCo
  .  .  .
Status                    Property   System.ServiceProcess.Service
```

> **TIP** By default, the Get-Member cmdlet does not show you the static methods and static properties of object classes. To get the static members of an object class, type get-member –static. For example, to get the static members of the ServiceProcess object, you'd enter get-service | get-member –static.

In the output, note that each facet of the Service object is listed by member type. You can make better sense of the list of available information when you filter for elements you want to see by adding the –MemberType parameter. The allowed values of –MemberType include

- AliasProperty, CodeProperty, NoteProperty, ParameterizedProperty, Property, PropertySet, ScriptProperty, CodeMethod, MemberSet, Method, and ScriptMethod, for examining elements of a particular type
- Properties, for examining all property-related elements
- Methods, for examining all method-related elements
- All, for examining all properties and methods (the default)

When you examine an object using Get-Member, note the alias properties. Aliases to properties work the same as other aliases. They're friendly names that you can use as shortcuts when you are working with an object.

Whereas Service objects have only one alias property (Name), most well-known objects have several alias properties. For example, Process objects have the alias properties shown in the following example and sample output:

```
get-process | get-member
```

```
    TypeName: System.Diagnostics.Process

Name                MemberType        Definition
----                ----------        ----------
Handles             AliasProperty     Handles = Handlecount
Name                AliasProperty     Name = ProcessName
NPM                 AliasProperty     NPM = NonpagedSystemMemory
PM                  AliasProperty     PM = PagedMemorySize
VM                  AliasProperty     VM = VirtualMemorySize
WS                  AliasProperty     WS = WorkingSet
```

And these aliases are displayed when you list running processes, as shown in the following example and sample output:

```
get-process
```

```
Handles  NPM(K)  PM(K)   WS(K) VM(M)   CPU(s)    Id ProcessName
-------  ------  -----   ----- -----   ------    -- -----------
     52       3   1296    3844    51     3.24  3004 acrotray
    139       4   2560    7344    75     6.11  1292 AlertService
    573      14  14680   11028   120     7.41  2764 aolsoftware
     97       4   2872    4476    53     8.02  1512 AppleMobil
```

When you type **get-process | get-member** and see that Process objects have dozens of other properties not listed, you might wonder what happened to these other properties and why they aren't listed. This occurs because PowerShell shows only streamlined views of well-known objects as part of the standard output. Typically, this output includes only the most important properties of an object.

PowerShell determines how to display an object of a particular type by using information stored in XML files that have names ending in .format.ps1xml. The formatting definitions for many well-known objects are in the types.ps1xml file. This file is stored in the $pshome directory.

The properties you don't see are still part of the object, and you have full access to them. For example, type **get-process winlogon | format-list – property ***, and you get complete details on every property of the Winlogon process by name and value.

Object Methods and Properties

Some methods and properties relate only to actual instances of an object, and this is why they are called *instance methods* and *instance properties*. The term *instance* is simply another word for *object*.

Often you will want to reference the methods and properties of objects through a variable in which the object is stored. To see how this works, consider the following example:

```
$myString = "THIS IS A TEST!"
```

Here, you store a character string in a variable named $myString. In PowerShell, the string is represented as a String object. String objects have a Length property that stores the length of the string. Therefore, you can determine the length of the string created previously by typing the following command:

```
$myString.Length
```

In this example, the length of the string is 15 characters, so the output is 15.

Although String objects have only one property, they have a number of methods, including ToUpper() and ToLower(). You use the ToUpper() method to display all the characters in the string in uppercase letters. You use the ToLower() method to display all the characters in the string in lowercase letters. For example, to change the previously created string to "this is a test!", you type the following command:

```
$myString.ToLower()
```

From these examples, you can see that you access a property of an object by placing a dot between the variable name that represents the object and the property name as shown here:

```
$ObjectName.PropertyName
$ObjectName.PropertyName = Value
```

And you can see that you access a method of an object by placing a dot between the variable name that represents the object and the method name, such as

```
$ObjectName.MethodName()
```

Because methods perform actions on objects, you often need to pass parameter values in the method call. The syntax for passing parameters in a method call is

```
$ObjectName.MethodName(parameter1, parameter2, …)
```

So far the techniques we've discussed for working with methods and properties are for actual instances of an object. However, you won't always be working with a tangible instance of an object. Sometimes, you'll want to work directly with the static methods and static properties that apply to a particular .NET Framework class type as a whole.

The .NET Framework includes a wide range of class types. Generally, .NET Framework class names are always enclosed in brackets. Examples of class type names include [System.Datetime], for working with dates and times, and [System.Diagnostics.Process], for working with system processes. However, PowerShell automatically prepends *System.* to type names, so you can also use [Datetime] for working with dates and times and [Diagnostics.Process] for working with system processes.

Static methods and static properties of a .NET Framework class are always available when you are working with an object class. However, if you try to display them with the Get-Member cmdlet, you won't see them unless you use the –Static parameter as well, such as

```
[System.Datetime] | get-member -Static
```

You access a static property of a .NET Framework class by placing two colon characters (::) between the bracketed class name and the property name as shown here:

```
[ClassName]::PropertyName
[ClassName]::PropertyName = Value
```

In this example, you use a static property of the [System.Datetime] class to display the current date and time:

```
[System.Datetime]::Now
Monday, February 15, 2017 11:05:22 PM
```

You access a static method of a .NET Framework class by placing two colon characters (::) between the bracketed class name and the method name, such as

```
[ClassName]::MethodName()
```

The syntax for passing parameters in a call to a static method is

```
[ClassName]::MethodName(parameter1, parameter2, …)
```

In this example, you use a static method of the [System.Diagnostics.Process] class to display information about a process:

```
[System.Diagnostics.Process]::GetProcessById(0)
Handles  NPM(K) PM(K)   WS(K) VM(M)  CPU(s)  Id ProcessName
-------  ------ -----   ----- -----  ------  -- -----------
      0       0     0      24     0   64.22   0 Idle
```

Object Types

By default, all object types that are used by PowerShell are defined in .ps1xml files in the $pshome directory. The default formatting and type files include the following:

- **Certificate.Format.ps1xml** Provides formatting guidelines for certificate objects and X.509 certificates
- **Diagnostics.Format.ps1xml** Provides formatting guidelines for objects created when you are working with performance counters and diagnostics in PowerShell
- **DotNetTypes.Format.ps1xml** Provides formatting guidelines for .NET Framework objects not covered in other formatting files, including CultureInfo, FileVersionInfo, and EventLogEntry objects

- **FileSystem.Format.ps1xml**   Provides formatting guidelines for file system objects
- **GetEvent.Types.ps1xml**   Provides formatting guidelines for event log configuration, event log records, and performance counters
- **Help.Format.ps1xml**   Provides formatting guidelines for the views PowerShell uses to display help file content
- **PowerShellCore.Format.ps1xml**   Provides formatting guidelines for objects that are created by the PowerShell core cmdlets
- **PowerShellTrace.Format.ps1xml**   Provides formatting guidelines for PSTraceSource objects generated when you are performing traces in PowerShell
- **Registry.Format.ps1xml**   Provides formatting guidelines for Registry objects
- **Types.ps1xml**   Provides formatting guidelines for System objects
- **WSMan.Format.ps1xml**   Provides formatting guidelines for objects created when you are working with WS Management configurations in PowerShell

PowerShell accomplishes automatic typing by using a common object that has the capability to state its type dynamically, add members dynamically, and interact with other objects through a consistent abstraction layer. This object is the PSObject. The PSObject can encapsulate any base object, whether it is a system object, a WMI object, a Component Object Model (COM) object, or an Active Directory Service Interfaces (ADSI) object.

By acting as a wrapper for an existing base object, the PSObject can be used to access adapted views of a base object or to extend a base object. Although an adapted view of a base object exposes only members that are directly accessible, you can access alternate views of a base object, and those alternate views can provide access to the extended members of a base object. Available views for base objects include the following:

- **PSBase** Used to access the original properties of the object without extension or adaptation
- **PSAdapted** Used to access an adapted view of the object
- **PSExtended** Used to access the extended properties and methods of the object that were added in the Types.ps1xml files or by using the Add-Member cmdlet
- **PSObject** Used to access the adapter that converts the base object to a PSObject
- **PSTypeNames** Used to access a list of types that describe the object

By default, PowerShell returns information only from the PSObject, PSExtended, and PSTypeNames views. However, you can use dot notation to access alternate views. In the following example, you obtain a Win32_Process object representing the winlogon.exe process:

```
$pr = Get-WmiObject Win32_Process | where-object {
$_.ProcessName -eq "winlogon.exe" }
```

If you then type **$pr** at the PowerShell prompt, you see all the information for this process from the PSObject, PSExtended, and PSTypeNames views. You can access the PSBase view to expose the members of the base object as shown in this example:

```
$pr.PSBase
```

Because there might be times when you want to extend an object yourself, you can do this using a custom Types.ps1xml file or by using the Add-Member cmdlet. The three most common extensions you'll want to use are

- **ScriptProperty** Allows you to add properties to types, including those that are based on a calculation
- **AliasProperty** Allows you to define an alias for a property
- **ScriptMethod** Allows you to define an action to take on an object

In custom Types.ps1xml files, you can define these extensions using XML elements, and there are many examples available in the $pshome directory. These extensions also can be added dynamically at the prompt or in your scripts. For example, a ScriptProperty is a type of object member that uses a block of code to process or extract information related to an object. The basic syntax is

```
$ObjectName | add-member -membertype scriptproperty
-name Name -value {CodeBlock}
```

Because the –Name and –Value parameters are position sensitive, you don't have to specify them explicitly. Knowing this, consider the following example and sample output:

```
$proc = get-process powershell;
$proc | add-member -Type scriptproperty "UpTime" {return
((date) - ($this.starttime))};
$proc | select Name, @{name='Uptime'; Expression={"{0:n0}" -
f $_.UpTime.TotalMinutes}};
```

```
Name                                      Uptime
----                                      ------
powershell                                   242
```

Here, you obtain a process object for any Powershell.exe processes running on the computer. You then use the Add-Member cmdlet to extend the standard process object by adding a ScriptProperty. The script block defined in the ScriptProperty is used to calculate the time that a process has been running. Then you get the process object and format its output to include the process name and new Uptime property. Using a regular expression, you convert the output value of the Uptime property to a value in minutes. The result is as shown.

What you don't see happening here is that the first time you assign a value to $proc, you are adding a collection of process objects. You then generate a second collection of process objects because you use the Add-Member cmdlet to wrap the original Process objects in a new PSObject instance that includes the new property you've defined.

While a ScriptProperty extends an object, an AliasProperty simply makes it easier to work with an object. To see how, let's access the C: drive using the Get-PSDrive cmdlet and then create a new PSDriveInfo object so that we can access information about the C: drive. Here's an example:

```
$myDrive = get-psdrive C
$myDriveInfo = New-Object System.IO.DriveInfo $myDrive
```

Now that you have an object you can work with, you can display information about the C: drive simply by typing **$myDriveInfo**. The output you see provides information about the drive, its status, its size, and its free space, and it will be similar to the following:

```
Name                 : C:\
DriveType            : Fixed
DriveFormat          : NTFS
IsReady              : True
AvailableFreeSpace   : 302748798976
TotalFreeSpace       : 302748798976
TotalSize            : 490580373504
RootDirectory        : C:\
VolumeLabel          : OS
```

Although the default format is a list, you can also view the information in table format, such as when you are working with multiple drives. When you type **$myDriveInfo | format-table –property ***, the output you get isn't pretty (unless you have a very wide console window). To clean up the output, you might want to create aliases for properties, such as AvailableFreeSpace, TotalFreeSpace, and RootDirectory. You can do this using the Add-Member cmdlet as well. The basic syntax is

```
$ObjectName | add-member -membertype aliasproperty -name
AliasName -value
PropertyName
```

where *ObjectName* is the name of the object you are working with, *AliasName* is the new alias for the property, and *PropertyName* is the original name of the property, such as

```
$myDriveInfo | add-member -membertype aliasproperty
-name Free -value AvailableFreeSpace

$myDriveInfo | add-member -membertype aliasproperty
-name Format -value DriveFormat
```

You can access an alias property as you would any other property. For example, to display the value of the AvailableFreeSpace property, you can type either

```
$myDriveInfo.AvailableFreeSpace
```

or

```
$myDriveInfo.Free
```

You can use alias properties in formatted output as well. An example is shown in the following command and sample output:

```
$myDriveInfo | format-table -property Name, Free, Format
```

```
Name                                    Free        Format
----                                    ----        ------
C:\                                     302748483584    NTFS
```

You use ScriptMethod extensions to define additional methods for an object. The basic syntax is

```
$ObjectName | add-member -membertype scriptmethod -name Name
  -value {CodeBlock}
```

Because the –Name and –Value parameters are position sensitive, you don't have to specify them explicitly. Knowing this, consider the following example:

```
$myDrive = get-psdrive C
```

```
$myDrive | add-member -membertype scriptmethod -name Remove
  -value { $force = [bool] $args[0];
  if ($force) {$this | Remove-PSDrive }
  else {$this | Remove-PSDrive -Confirm}
}
```

Here you define a Remote method for a PSDrive object. If you call the method without passing any argument values, PowerShell prompts you to confirm that you want to remove the drive from the current session. If you call the method and pass $true or 0 (zero) as the first argument, PowerShell removes the drive from the current session without requiring confirmation.

Digging Deeper into Objects

To dig a bit deeper into objects, let's look at the $host object. You can use the PowerShell console's Properties dialog box to specify the options, fonts, layouts, and colors to use. The $host object also gives you access to the underlying user interface, which can be either the PowerShell console or the PowerShell application.

To view the current settings of the $host object, type the following command:

```
$host.ui.rawui | format-list -property *
```

The output you see will be similar to the following:

```
ForegroundColor        : DarkYellow
BackgroundColor        : DarkMagenta
CursorPosition         : 0,1050
WindowPosition         : 0,1001
CursorSize             : 25
BufferSize             : 120,3000
WindowSize             : 120,50
MaxWindowSize          : 120,95
MaxPhysicalWindowSize  : 240,95
KeyAvailable           : False
WindowTitle            : Windows PowerShell
```

In the output, you see a number of properties, including the following:

- ForegroundColor, which sets the color of the prompt and text
- BackgroundColor, which sets the background color of the window
- WindowTitle, which sets the name of the PowerShell window

To work with the PowerShell window, you must obtain a reference to the $host object. The easiest way to do this is to store the $host object in a variable, such as

```
$myHostWin = $host.ui.rawui
```

After you have a reference to an object, you can work with the object through the available properties and methods. You can set the foreground or background color to any of the following default color values:

- Black, DarkBlue, DarkGreen, DarkCyan
- DarkRed, DarkMagenta, DarkYellow, Gray
- DarkGray, Blue, Green, Cyan
- Red, Magenta, Yellow, White

To do so, reference the host window object with the property name and the desired value, such as

```
$myHostWin.ForegroundColor = "White"
```

or

```
$myHostWin.BackgroundColor = "DarkGray"
```

Similarly, you can use the WindowTitle property to specify the title for the window. Here's an example:

```
$myHostWin.WindowTitle = "PowerShell on $env.computername"
```

Here, you set the window title to a value based on the computer name. Thus, if you are logged on to TechPC32, the window title is set to

```
PowerShell on TechPC32
```

Take a look back at the output values for the properties of the $host object. Several of properties have values separated by commas. This tells you the value is an array of subproperties. To view the subproperties of a property, you can examine that property separately and format the output as a list. For example, to examine the subproperties of CursorPosition, you can type the following command:

```
$host.ui.rawui.CursorPosition | format-list -property *
```

The output will look similar to the following:

```
X : 0
Y : 2999
```

This tells you the CursorPosition property has two subproperties: X and Y. You reference subproperties of properties by extending the dot notation as shown in these examples:

```
$host.ui.rawui.CursorPosition.X
```

or

```
$host.ui.rawui.CursorPosition.Y
```

If you continue examining subproperties of properties, you'll find both CursorPosition and WindowPosition have X and Y subproperties. You'll also find that BufferSize, WindowSize, MaxWindowSize, and MaxPhysicalWindowSize have Width and Height properties.

After you know what the subproperties are, you can examine their values in the same way you examine the values of standard properties. However, in this case the subproperties cannot be set directly; you must create an instance of the $host object using the New-Object cmdlet and then modify the properties of the object instance.

This means you must first get a reference to the $host object as shown here:

```
$myHost = $host.ui.rawui
```

Then you create a new object instance and set the desired subproperties on the new instance as shown here:

```
$myHostWindowSize = New-Object
System.Management.Automation.Host.Size(150,100)
```

In this example, you dynamically set the host window size. The first value passed is the desired width. The second value passed is the desired height.

Chapter 15. Working with COM and .NET Framework Objects

The Component Object Model (COM) and the .NET Framework are two object models you'll work with frequently in PowerShell. Although many applications provide scripting and administrative objects through COM, .NET Framework and even PowerShell cmdlets are becoming increasingly prevalent.

Creating and Using COM Objects

You can create instances of COM objects using the New-Object cmdlet. The basic syntax is

```
New-Object [-Set AssocArray] [-Strict] [-ComObject] String
```

When creating the object, set the –ComObject parameter to the object's programmatic identifier (ProgID). Most well-known COM objects can be used within PowerShell, including those for Windows Script Host (WSH). The following example creates a shortcut on your desktop:

```
$spath = "$Home\Desktop\PowerShellHome.lnk"
$WshShell = New-Object -ComObject WScript.Shell
$scut = $WshShell.CreateShortcut($spath)
$scut.TargetPath = $PSHome
$scut.Save()
```

This shortcut is called *PowerShellHome*, and it links to the $PSHome directory.

> **TIP** After you've attached to a COM object, you can use tab expansion to view available options. For example, if $a is your object, type **$a.** and then press Tab or Shift+Tab to browse available methods and properties.

140

Beyond WSH, there are many other COM objects you can use. Table 15-1 lists some of these by their ProgID.

TABLE 15-1 Common COM Objects for Use with Windows PowerShell

PROGID	DESCRIPTION
Access.Application	Accesses Microsoft Office Access
CEnroll.Cenroll	Accesses certificate enrollment services
Excel.Application	Accesses Microsoft Office Excel
Excel.Sheet	Accesses worksheets in Excel
HNetCfg.FwMgr	Accesses Windows Firewall
InternetExplorer.Application	Accesses Internet Explorer
MAPI.Session	Accesses Messaging Application Programming Interface (MAPI) sessions
Microsoft.Update.AutoUpdate	Accesses the autoupdate schedule for Microsoft Update
Microsoft.Update.Installer	Allows you to install updates from Microsoft Update
Microsoft.Update.Searches	Allows you to search for updates from Microsoft Update
Microsoft.Update.Session	Accesses the update history for Microsoft Update

PROGID	DESCRIPTION
Microsoft.Update.SystemInfo	Accesses system information for Microsoft Update
Outlook.Application	Accesses Microsoft Office Outlook
OutlookExpress.MessageList	Allows for automation of e-mail in Microsoft Office Outlook Express
PowerPoint.Application	Accesses Microsoft Office PowerPoint
Publisher.Application	Accesses Microsoft Office Publisher
SAPI.SpVoice	Accesses the Microsoft Speech application programming interface (API)
Scripting.FileSystemObject	Accesses the computer's file system
SharePoint.OpenDocuments	Accesses Microsoft SharePoint Services
Shell.Application	Accesses the File Explorer shell
Shell.LocalMachine	Accesses information about the Windows shell on the local computer
SQLDMO.SQLServer	Accesses the management features of Microsoft SQL Server
WMPlayer.OCX	Accesses Windows Media Player

PROGID	DESCRIPTION
Word.Application	Accesses Microsoft Office Word
Word.Document	Accesses documents in Word

To show you how easy it is to work with COM objects, I'll work through a series of basic examples with File Explorer, Internet Explorer, and Excel. The following example creates an instance of the File Explorer shell and then uses its Windows() method to display the location name of all open instances of File Explorer and Internet Explorer:

```
$shell = new-object -comobject shell.application
$shell.windows() | select-object locationname
```

```
Data
This PC
Network
```

By piping the output to Select-Object LocationName, you display the value of the LocationName property for each shell object. File Explorer windows are listed by name or folder, such as Computer or Network. Internet Explorer windows are listed by Web page title. With Internet Explorer 11 and later, you get a listing for each page opened in a tabbed window as well. You get details about both File Explorer and Internet Explorer because both applications use the File Explorer shell.

If you want to know all the properties available for each shell object, pipe the output to Select-Object without specifying properties to display, as shown in this example and sample output:

```
$shell = new-object -comobject shell.application
$shell.windows() | select-object
```

Application	: System.__ComObject
Parent	: System.__ComObject
Container	:
Document	: mshtml.HTMLDocumentClass
TopLevelContainer	: True
Type	: HTML Document
Left	: 959
Top	: 1
Width	: 961
Height	: 1169
LocationName	: Windows Nation: Home of Tech Author
William Stanek	
LocationURL	: http://www.williamstanek.com/
Busy	: False
Name	: Windows Internet Explorer
HWND	: 854818
FullName	: C:\Program Files\Internet
Explorer\iexplore.exe	
Path	: C:\Program Files\Internet Explorer\
Visible	: True
StatusBar	: True
StatusText	: Done
ToolBar	: 1
MenuBar	: True
FullScreen	: False
ReadyState	: 4
Offline	: False
Silent	: False
RegisterAsBrowser	: False
RegisterAsDropTarget	: True
TheaterMode	: False
AddressBar	: True
Resizable	: True

REAL WORLD Some COM objects have a .NET Framework wrapper that connects them to the .NET Framework. Because the behavior of the wrapper might be different from the behavior of the normal COM object, New-Object has a –Strict parameter to warn you about wrappers. When you use this flag, PowerShell displays a warning message to tell you that you are not working with a standard COM object. The COM object is still created, however.

The following example opens Internet Explorer to *www.williamstanek.com*:

```
$iexp = new-object -comobject "InternetExplorer.Application"
$iexp.navigate("www.williamstanek.com")
$iexp.visible = $true
```

Here, you create a new COM object for Internet Explorer. The new object has the same properties as those for the shell window listed previously. You use the Navigate() method to set the location to browse and the Visible property to display the window. To see a list of all methods and properties you can work with, enter the example and then type **$iexp | get-member**. You can call any method listed as shown in the example. You can modify properties that you can get and set.

The following example accesses the Microsoft Speech API and talks to you:

```
$v = new-object -comobject "SAPI.SPVoice"
$v.speak("Well, hello there. How are you?")
```

Here, you create a new COM object for the Speech API. You use the Speak() method to say something. To see a list of all methods and properties you can work with, enter the example and then enter $v | get-member. You can call any method listed as shown in the example. You can modify any property that you can get and set.

The following example works with Microsoft Excel:

```
$a = New-Object -comobject "Excel.Application"
$a.Visible = $True
```

```
$wb = $a.workbooks.add()
$ws = $wb.worksheets.item(1)

$ws.cells.item(1,1) = "Computer Name"
$ws.cells.item(1,2) = "Location"
$ws.cells.item(1,3) = "OS Type"
$ws.cells.item(2,1) = "TechPC84"
$ws.cells.item(2,2) = "5th Floor"
$ws.cells.item(2,3) = "Windows 8.1"

$a.activeworkbook.saveas("c:\data\myws.xls")
```

Here, you create a new COM object for Excel and then you display the Excel window by setting the Visible property. When you instantiate the Excel object, you have a number of methods and properties available for working with the Excel application and a number of related subobjects that represent workbooks, worksheets, and individual table cells. To view the default values for properties of the Excel object, enter the example and then enter **$a**. To view the methods and properties available for working with the top-level Excel application object, enter **$a | get-member**.

After you create the Excel object, you add a workbook to the application window by using the Add() method of the Workbooks object. This creates a Workbook object, which also has methods and properties as well as a related Worksheets object array. To view the default values for properties of the Workbook object, enter **$wb**. To view the methods and properties available for working with the Workbook object, type **$wb | get-member**.

Next, you specify that you want to work with the first worksheet in the workbook you just created. You do this by using the Item() method of the Worksheets object array. This creates a Worksheet object, which also has methods and properties as well as a related Cells object array. To view the default values for properties of the Worksheet object, enter **$ws**. To view the methods and properties available for working with the Worksheet object, enter **$ws | get-member**.

Once you've created a worksheet, you can add data to the worksheet. You do this by using the Item() method of the Cells object array. When you call the Item() method, you specify the column and row position of the cell you want to write to and then specify the value you want. To view the default values for properties of the Cells object, enter **$ws.cells**. To view the methods and properties available for working with the Cells object, enter **$ws.cells | get-member**.

Individual table cells are represented by Cell objects. To view the default values for properties of the cell in column 1 row 1, enter **$ws.cells.item(1,1)**. To view the methods and properties available for working with the Cell object in column 1 row 1, enter **$ws.cells.item(1,1) | get-member**.

Working with .NET Framework Classes and Objects

The .NET Framework is so tightly integrated with PowerShell that it is difficult to talk about PowerShell and not talk about .NET as well. We've used .NET classes and .NET objects in this and other chapters.

One way to instantiate and use a .NET Framework object is to make a direct invocation to a static class. To do this, you enclose the class name in square brackets, insert two colon characters, and then add a method or property call. This is the same technique we previously used to work with instances of [System.Datetime], [System.Math], and other classes.

The following example creates an instance of the [System.Environment] class and gets the current directory:

```
[system.environment]::CurrentDirectory
```

```
C:\data\scripts\myscripts
```

> **TIP** You can use tab expansion to view static members of a .NET Framework class. Type the class name in brackets, type **::** and then press Tab or Shift+Tab to browse available methods and properties.

You also can create a reference to an instance of a .NET Framework object using the New-Object cmdlet. The basic syntax is

```
New-Object [-Set AssocArray] [-TypePath Strings]
[[-ArgumentList] Objects] [-TypeName] String
```

The following example creates a reference object for the Application log through the System.Diagnostic.Eventlog object:

```
$log = new-object -type system.diagnostics.eventlog
-argumentlist application
```

```
Max(K) Retain OverflowAction       Entries Name
------ ------ --------------       ------- ----
20,480      0 OverwriteAsNeeded     45,061 application
```

> **TIP** After you've attached to a .NET Framework class instance, you can use tab expansion to view instance members. For example, if you store the object in $log, you type **$log,** type a dot (**.**), and then press Tab or Shift+Tab to browse available methods and properties.

Although we've looked at many .NET Framework classes previously, there are many more available. Table 15-2 lists some of these by their class name.

TABLE 15-2 Common .NET Framework Objects for Use with Windows PowerShell

CLASS	DESCRIPTION
Microsoft.Win32.Registry	Provides Registry objects for working with root keys
Microsoft.Win32.RegistryKey	Represents keys in the registry
System.AppDomain	Represents the environment where applications execute
System.Array	Provides interaction with arrays
System.Console	Represents the standard input, output, and error streams for the console
System.Convert	Provides static methods and a property for converting data types
System.Datetime	Represents a datetime value
System.Diagnostics.Debug	Provides methods and properties for debugging
System.Diagnostics.EventLog	Provides interaction with Windows event logs
System.Diagnostics.Process	Provides interaction with Windows processes
System.Drawing.Bitmap	Represents pixel data for images

CLASS	DESCRIPTION
System.Drawing.Image	Provides methods and properties for working with images
System.Environment	Provides information about the working environment and platform
System.Guid	Represents a globally unique identifier (GUID)
System.IO.Stream	Represents IO streams
System.Management.Automation.PowerShell	Represents a PowerShell object to which you can add notes, properties, and so on
System.Math	Provides static methods and properties for performing mathematical functions
System.Net.Dns	Provides interaction with Domain Name System (DNS)
System.Net.NetworkCredential	Provides credentials for network authentication
System.Net.WebClient	Provides interaction with the Web client
System.Random	Represents a random number generator
System.Reflection.Assembly	Represents .NET Framework assemblies so that you can load and work with them

CLASS	DESCRIPTION
System.Security.Principal. WellKnownSidType	Represents security identifiers (SIDs)
System.Security.Principal. WindowsBuiltInRole	Specifies built-in roles
System.Security.Principal. WindowsIdentity	Represents a Windows user
System.Security.Principal. WindowsPrincipal	Allows checking of a user's group membership
System.Security.SecureString	Represents secure text that is encrypted for privacy
System.String	Provides interaction with strings
System.Text.RegularExpressions.Regex	Represents immutable regular expressions
System.Threading.Thread	Provides interaction with threads
System.Type	Represents type declarations
System.Uri	Represents uniform resource identifiers (URIs)
System.Windows.Forms. FlowLayoutPanel	Represents a layout panel

CLASS	DESCRIPTION
System.Windows.Forms.Form	Represents a window or dialog box in an application

Some .NET Framework objects require that related .NET Framework assemblies be loaded before you can use them. Assemblies are simply sets of files, which can include dynamic-link libraries (DLLs), EXE files, and other resources that the .NET Framework object needs to work properly. You'll know that a .NET Framework object requires an assembly because PowerShell will throw an error if the assembly is not loaded, such as

```
Unable to find type [system.drawing.image]: make sure that
the assembly
containing this type is loaded.
At line:1 char:23
+ [system.drawing.image] <<<< |get-member -static
    + CategoryInfo          : InvalidOperation:
(system.drawing.image:String)
[], RuntimeException
    + FullyQualifiedErrorId : TypeNotFound
```

The solution is to use the [Reflection.Assembly] class to load the required assemblies. One way to do this is with the LoadWithPartialName() method of the Reflection.Assembly class. The syntax is

```
[Reflection.Assembly]::LoadWithPartialName("ClassName")
```

where *ClassName* is the name of the .NET Framework class that completes the requirement. For example, you can use the System.Drawing.Bitmap class to convert a GIF image to JPEG. Because this class requires the assemblies of the System.Windows.Forms class, you must load the related assemblies before you can convert an image.

When you load a reflection assembly, PowerShell confirms this and displays the related output automatically as shown in this example:

```
[Reflection.Assembly]::LoadWithPartialName
("System.Windows.Forms")
```

```
GAC     Version            Location
---     -------            --------
True    v4.0.30319  C:\Windows\assembly\GAC_MSIL\
System.Windows.Forms \v4.0_4.0.0.0__b77a5c561934e089\
System.Windows.For...
```

This output is important. The True value for GAC tells you the assembly loaded successfully. The Version value tells you the specific version of .NET Framework the assembly uses. The location tells you the location in the operating system.

When you call a reflection assembly, I recommend formatting the output as a list as shown in this example:

```
[Reflection.Assembly]::LoadWithPartialName
("System.Windows.Forms") | format-list
```

```
CodeBase :
file:///C:/Windows/assembly/GAC_MSIL/System.Windows.Forms/
4.0_4.0.0.0__b77a5c561934e089/System.Windows.Forms.dll
EntryPoint :
EscapedCodeBase :
file:///C:/Windows/assembly/GAC_MSIL/System.Windows.
Forms/4.0_4.0.0.0__b77a5c561934e089/System.Windows.Forms.dll
FullName   : System.Windows.Forms, Version=4.0.0.0,
Culture=neutral, PublicKeyToken=b77a5c561934e089
GlobalAssemblyCache   : True
HostContext           : 0
ImageFileMachine      :
```

```
ImageRuntimeVersion      : v4.0.303139
Location                 :
C:\Windows\assembly\GAC_MSIL\System.Windows.Forms\4.0_4.0.0.
0__b77a5c561934e089\System.Windows.Forms.dll
ManifestModule           : System.Windows.Forms.dll
MetadataToken            :
PortableExecutableKind   :
ReflectionOnly           : False
```

This listing gives you important additional details about the assembly you just loaded, including the simple text name, version number, culture identifier, and public key. All of this information is listed as the FullName entry. If you copy the FullName entry exactly, beginning with the simple text name, you have the full load string you need to use the Load() method. Because the Load() method is the preferred way to load assemblies and the LoadWithPartialName() method is deprecated, this will help you prepare for when you can no longer use the LoadWithPartialName() method.

To continue the example, after you've loaded the [System.Windows.Forms] class, you can convert a GIF image in the current directory to JPEG using the following statements:

```
$image = New-Object System.Drawing.Bitmap myimage.gif
$image.Save("mynewimage.jpg","JPEG")
```

Here, you get an image called MyImage.gif in the current directory and then convert the image to JPEG format. You can substitute any GIF image and add an image path as necessary. While you are working with the image, you can view its width, height, and other properties by entering **$image**. You can view methods for working with the image by entering **$image | get-member**.

Chapter 16. Performing WMI Queries

Windows Management Instrumentation (WMI) is a management framework that you can use to query a computer to determine its attributes. For example, you can create a WMI query to determine the operating system running on a computer or the amount of available memory. WMI queries by themselves are helpful, especially when used in scripts.

You can use WMI queries to examine settings based on just about any measurable characteristic of a computer, including

- Amount of memory installed
- Available hard disk space
- Processor type or speed
- Network adapter type or speed
- Operating system version, service pack level, or hotfix
- Registry key or key value
- System services that are running

You create WMI queries using the WMI Query Language. The basic syntax is

```
Select * from WMIObjectClass where Condition
```

In this syntax, *WMIObjectClass* is the WMI object class you want to work with, and *Condition* is the condition you want to evaluate. The Select statement returns objects of the specified class. A condition has three parts:

- The name of the object property you are examining

- An operator, such as = for equals, > for greater than, or < for less than
- The value to evaluate

Operators can also be defined by using Is or Like. The Is operator is used to exactly match criteria. The Like condition is used to match a keyword or text string within a value. In the following example, you create a query to look for computers running Windows 8.1 or Windows Server 2012 R2:

```
Select * from Win32_OperatingSystem where Version like
"%6.3%"
```

The Win32_OperatingSystem class tracks the overall operating system configuration. The Win32_OperatingSystem class is one of two WMI object classes that you'll use frequently. The other is Win32_ComputerSystem. The Win32_ComputerSystem class tracks the overall computer configuration.

In Windows PowerShell, you can use the Get-WMIObject cmdlet to get a WMI object that you want to work with. The basic syntax is

```
Get-WmiObject -Class WMIClass -Namespace NameSpace
-ComputerName ComputerName
```

where *WMIClass* is the WMI class you want to work with, *NameSpace* sets the namespace to use within WMI, and *ComputerName* sets the name of the computer to work with.

When working with WMI, you should work with the root namespace, as specified by setting the –Namespace parameter to root/cimv2. By using the –Computer parameter, you can specify the computer you want to work with. If you want to work with the local computer, use a dot (.)

instead of a computer name. By redirecting the object to Format-List *, you can list all the properties of the object and their values.

Following this, you can examine the Win32_OperatingSystem object and its properties to obtain summary information regarding the operating system configuration of a computer by typing the following command at the Windows PowerShell prompt:

```
Get-WmiObject -Class Win32_OperatingSystem -Namespace
root/cimv2  -ComputerName .  | Format-List *
```

To save the output in a file, simply redirect the output to a file. In the following example, you redirect the output to a file in the working directory named os_save.txt:

```
Get-WmiObject -Class Win32_OperatingSystem -Namespace
root/cimv2 -ComputerName .  | Format-List * > os_save.txt
```

The detailed operating system information tells you a great deal about the operating system running on the computer. The same is true for computer configuration details, which can be obtained by typing the following command at a Windows PowerShell prompt:

```
Get-WmiObject -Class Win32_ComputerSystem -Namespace
root/cimv2 -ComputerName .  | Format-List *
```

In addition to targeting operating system or computer configuration properties, you might want to target computers based on the amount of disk space and file system type. In the following example, you target computers that have more than 100 megabytes (MB) of available space on the C, D, or G partition:

```
get-wmiobject -query 'Select * from Win32_LogicalDisk where
(Name = "C:" OR Name = "D:"  OR Name = "G:" ) AND DriveType
= 3 AND FreeSpace > 104857600 AND FileSystem = "NTFS"'
```

In the preceding example, *DriveType = 3* represents a local disk, and
FreeSpace units are in bytes (100 MB = 104,857,600 bytes). The partitions
must be located on one or more local fixed disks, and they must be
running the NTFS file system. Note that while PowerShell understands
storage units in MB, KB, or whatever, the WMI query language does not.

In Windows PowerShell, you can examine all the properties of the
Win32_LogicalDisk object by typing the following command at the
Windows PowerShell prompt:

```
Get-WmiObject -Class Win32_LogicalDisk -Namespace root/cimv2
-ComputerName . | Format-List *
```

As you'll see, there are many properties you can work with, including
Compressed, which indicates whether a disk is compressed. Table 16-1
provides an overview of these and other important WMI object classes.

TABLE 16-1 WMI Classes Commonly Used with Windows PowerShell

WMI CLASS	DESCRIPTIONS
Win32_BaseBoard	Represents the motherboard
Win32_BIOS	Represents the attributes of the computer's firmware
Win32_BootConfiguration	Represents the computer's boot configuration
Win32_CacheMemory	Represents cache memory on the computer

WMI CLASS	DESCRIPTIONS
Win32_CDROMDrive	Represents each CD-ROM drive configured on the computer
Win32_ComputerSystem	Represents a computer system in a Windows environment
Win32_Desktop	Represents the common characteristics of a user's desktop
Win32_DesktopMonitor	Represents the type of monitor or display device connected to the computer
Win32_DiskDrive	Represents each physical disk drive on a computer
Win32_DiskPartition	Represents each partitioned area of a physical disk
Win32_DiskQuota	Tracks disk space usage for NTFS volumes
Win32_Environment	Represents a system environment setting on a computer
Win32_LogicalDisk	Represents each logical disk device used for data storage
Win32_LogonSession	Provides information about the current logon session

WMI CLASS	DESCRIPTIONS
Win32_NetworkAdapter	Represents each network adapter on the computer
Win32_NetworkAdapterConfiguration	Represents the configuration of each network adapter on the computer
Win32_NetworkConnection	Represents an active network connection
Win32_OperatingSystem	Represents the working environment for the operating system
Win32_OSRecoveryConfiguration	Represents recovery and dump files
Win32_PageFileUsage	Represents the page file used for handling virtual memory swapping
Win32_PhysicalMemory	Represents each DIMM of physical memory configured on the computer
Win32_PhysicalMemoryArray	Represents the total memory configuration of the computer by capacity and number of memory devices
Win32_Printer	Represents each configured print device on the computer
Win32_PrinterConfiguration	Represents configuration details for print devices

WMI CLASS	DESCRIPTIONS
Win32_PrintJob	Represents active print jobs generated by applications
Win32_Processor	Represents each processor or processor core on the computer
Win32_QuickFixEngineeering	Represents updates that have been applied to the computer
Win32_Registry	Represents the Windows registry
Win32_SCSIController	Represents each SCSI controller on the computer
Win32_Service	Represents each service configured on the computer
Win32_Share	Represents each file share configured on the computer
Win32_SoundDevice	Represents the computer's sound device

Using the techniques I discussed previously, you can examine the properties of any or all of these objects in Windows PowerShell. If you do, you will find that Win32_PhysicalMemoryArray has a MaxCapacity property that tracks the total physical memory in kilobytes. Knowing this, you can easily create a WMI query to look for computers with 256 MB of RAM or more. The WMI query to handle the task is the following:

```
if (get-wmiobject -query "Select * from
Win32_PhysicalMemoryArray where
MaxCapacity > 262000") {write-host $env:computername}
```

CORPC87

I used the value 262000 because there are 262,144 kilobytes in 256 MB, and we want the computer to have at least this capacity. Now if you add this statement to a job running on remote computers as discussed in Chapter 12, "Creating Background Jobs," you can search across the enterprise to find computers that meet your specifications.

To display a complete list of WMI objects, type the following command at the Windows PowerShell prompt:

```
Get-WmiObject –list -Namespace root/cimv2 -ComputerName . |
Format-List name
```

Because the list of available objects is so long, you'll definitely want to redirect the output to a file. In the following example, you redirect the output to a file in the working directory called FullWMIObjectList.txt:

```
Get-WmiObject –list -Namespace root/cimv2 -ComputerName . |
Format-List name > FullWMIObjectList.txt
```

Rather than viewing all WMI classes, you might want to see only the Win32 WMI classes. To view only the Win32 WMI classes, use the following command:

```
Get-WmiObject -list | where {$_.name -like "*Win32_*"}
```

Chapter 17. Performing MI Queries in CIM Sessions

Common Information Model (CIM) describes the structure and behavior of managed resources. As discussed in Chapter 10, "Establishing CIM Sessions," WMI is a CIMOM server service that implements the CIM standard on Windows, and you can use CIM cmdlets to work with MI objects. You typically work with CIM objects on remote computers via CIM sessions.

When managing remote computers, you may find that working with CIM cmdlets is easier than working with WMI cmdlets. A key reason for this is that the CIM cmdlets make it easier to discover and work with Windows resources and components.

Working within CIM sessions is also much more efficient than performing individual MI queries. Why? When you establish a persistent CIM session, you work within the context of this session, and your management computer and the remote computers you are working with don't need to repeatedly establish, provision and remove connections.

How CIM makes Windows resources and components easier to work with is primarily through Get-CimClass, which makes it easy to discover available MI classes. For example, you can enter **Get-CimClass** to list every available MI object.

When you are working with CIM, not only are the WMI classes discussed previously available but so are generalized CIM classes. For example, Win32_OperatingSystem is a WMI class for working with Windows operating systems while CIM_OperatingSystem is a generalized MI class for working with any operating system that supports CIM.

CIM also gives you more options for working with related objects. For example, not only can you work with CIM_OperatingSystem, but you also can work with CIM_InstalledOS.

If you find a specific MI object that you want to work with, such as Win32_DiskDrive or Win32_LogicalDisk, you can use Get-CimClass to examine available methods and properties. In the following example, you work with Win32_LogicalDisk and display its methods and properties:

```
$dd = get-cimclass win32_logicaldisk
$dd.cimclassmethods
$dd.cimclassproperties
```

The methods available include: SetPowerState, Reset, Chkdsk, ScheduleAutoChk, and ExcludeFromAutochk. The properties available include: Caption, Description, InstallDate, Name, Status, Availability, DeviceID, ErrorDescription, LastErrorCode, PowerManagementCapabilities, and more.

> **NOTE**   With CIM cmdlets, the default namespace is root/cimv2.). Thus, unless you specify a different namespace to work with, the root/cimv2 namespace is used.

When you know the methods and properties of an object class, you can then more easily work with related instances of that object class. The cmdlet you use to work with instances of an object class is Get-CimInstance. The basic syntax for Get-CimInstance is:

```
Get-CimInstance -Class ClassName
```

Where ClassName is the name of the MI class you want to examine. In the following example, you store instances of Win32_LogicalDisk in the $dd variable and then list them:

```
$dd = get-ciminstance -class win32_logicaldisk
$dd | fl
```

And the result is output similar to the following:

```
DeviceID     : C:
DriveType    : 3
ProviderName :
FreeSpace    : 196397465600
Size         : 254779846656
VolumeName   : OS

DeviceID     : D:
DriveType    : 3
ProviderName :
FreeSpace    : 8478121984
Size         : 8518627328
VolumeName   : Data
```

Here, note that there are two logical disks on the computer. While the standard properties that are displayed include DeviceID, DriveType, FreeSpace, Size and VolumeName, there are many other available properties that you can work with including: BlockSize, NumberOfBlocks, Compressed, FileSystem, and QuotasDisabled.

You can easily display the value of any property. For example, if you wanted to identify the filesystems used by these logical drives, you would enter:

```
$dd = get-ciminstance -class win32_logicaldisk
$dd.filesystem
```

The resulting output shows the filesystem associated with each logical drive, such as:

```
NTFS
NTFS
```

Rather than working with all instances of an object, you'll often want to examine specific instances of an object, such as only the C drive rather than both the C and D drives. There are several ways you can do this. The first approach is to user a filter and the basic syntax is:

```
Get-CimInstance –Class ClassName –Filter Condition
```

Where *ClassName* is the name of the MI class you want to examine and *Condition* specifies the condition to evaluate and use as a filter. Conditions with Get-CimInstance work the same as discussed previously in "Performing WMI Queries." Consider the following example:

```
$dd = get-ciminstance -class win32_logicaldisk
-filter 'deviceid = "c:"'
```

Here, you use a filter to specify that you only want to examine the logical disk with the DeviceID of C:.

Another way to work with specific instances of an object is to filter using a query and the basic syntax is:

```
Get-CimInstance –Query Query
```

Where *Query* specifies the query string to use as a filter. Query strings with Get-CimInstance work the same as discussed previously in "Performing WMI Queries."

As with WMI, you can use CIM queries to examine settings based on just about any measurable characteristic of a computer. Consider the following example:

```
$dd = get-ciminstance -query 'Select * from
Win32_OperatingSystem where Version like "%6.3%"'
```

Here, you create a query to look for computers running Windows 8.1 or Windows Server 2012 R2.

About the Author

William Stanek (http://www.williamstanek.com/) has more than 20 years of hands-on experience with advanced programming and development. He is a leading technology expert, an award-winning author, and a pretty-darn-good instructional trainer. Over the years, his practical advice has helped millions of programmers, developers, and network engineers all over the world. His current and books include *Windows 8.1 Administration Pocket Consultants*, *Windows Server 2012 R2 Pocket Consultants* and *Windows Server 2012 R2 Inside Outs*.

William has been involved in the commercial Internet community since 1991. His core business and technology experience comes from more than 11 years of military service. He has substantial experience in developing server technology, encryption, and Internet solutions. He has written many technical white papers and training courses on a wide variety of topics. He frequently serves as a subject matter expert and consultant.

William has an MS with distinction in information systems and a BS in computer science, magna cum laude. He is proud to have served in the Persian Gulf War as a combat crewmember on an electronic warfare aircraft. He flew on numerous combat missions into Iraq and was awarded nine medals for his wartime service, including one of the United States of America's highest flying honors, the Air Force Distinguished Flying Cross. Currently, he resides in the Pacific Northwest with his wife and children.

William recently rediscovered his love of the great outdoors. When he's not writing, he can be found hiking, biking, backpacking, traveling, or trekking in search of adventure with his family!

Find William on Twitter at www.twitter.com/WilliamStanek and on Facebook at www.facebook.com/William.Stanek.Author.